At the Bamboo Bar

At the Bamboo Bar

A Birthday Bash at the Most
Celebrated Saloon in Bangkok

Morgan McFinn

ASIA BOOKS

Published and Distributed by
Asia Books Co. Ltd.,
5 Sukhumvit Road Soi 61,
PO Box 40,
Bangkok 10110,
Thailand.
Tel: (66) 0-2715-9000 ext. 3202–4
Fax: (66) 0-2714-2799
E-mail: information@asiabooks.com
Website: www.asiabooks.com

© Morgan McFinn, 2002

All rights reserved. No part of this publication may be reprinted or reproduced, stored in a retrieval system, or transmitted in any form or by any means, mechanical, electronic, photocopying, recording, or otherwise, without prior permission in writing from the publisher.

This book is a work of fiction. All names, characters, and other elements of the story are either the product of the author's imagination or else are used only fictitiously. Any resemblance to real characters, living or dead, or to real incidents is entirely coincidental.

Typeset by COMSET Limited Partnership
Printed by Darnsutha Press Ltd.

ISBN 974-8303-69-7

*To the memory of young Johnny Dolan,
and
in honor of his family who loved him so well.*

Acknowledgements

Richard Baker, Jonathan Haid, Period.

This is going to be a story about an evening I spent at the Bamboo Bar in the Oriental Hotel commemorating my fiftieth birthday. It was sort of a surprise party. I had invited several of my Bangkok friends to join me. None of them showed up. I was really surprised.

First of all, it's my birthday. That is to say, it is the *anniversary* of my birthday—the fiftieth anniversary, to be exact. I am fifty years old today—half a century. Many people claim that that is a rather significant milestone, but in terms of longevity it doesn't really amount to much these days. Your typical ne'er-do-well can smoke two packs of cigarettes and drink half a bottle of Scotch a day and still fairly well stagger by the fifty-year marker. I mean, it's not like we're wearing loincloths trying to eke out a livelihood in a Borneo jungle full of venomous snakes, wild beasts, and angry Dayaks.

Given the advances of medical science, if a person doesn't live to be fifty years old today, it's more than likely a case of some freakish incident. Of course, I'm referring to those people who have access to and can afford the services of these medical advances. Nevertheless, the way things are going, it is conceivable that in twenty years or so the three leading causes of death will be accidents, homicide, and suicide.

All of these causes reflect a certain degree of fatigue. Accidents are usually a result of carelessness often prompted by fatigue. As for homicide and suicide . . . well, someone has either grown menacingly tired of us or we've simply grown weary of ourselves. In my case, I've been living alone for much of my adult life, and by most standards of reference am unemployed. There really aren't any people who have had occasion to become especially annoyed with me, and for the most part I enjoy my own company. I honestly think that enjoying one's own company is a key factor in achieving longevity. Many people who know me are amazed how I manage to do this, but I suspect that some of those people are just jealous and enjoy insulting me. God only knows why! Then again, speaking of accidents, I don't suppose it is one that I end up spending most of my time alone.

Sometimes people sabotage their own health; induce their own illness, simply to get attention. Now, these are really sick people. I guess they enjoy feeling sorry for themselves. Make public spectacles of themselves wallowing in their own miserable, stinking puddles of emotional puke, self-pity, and spiritual nausea. What a joy they are to be around.

While in the process of transcribing the events of this special evening, I was once again banging my head against a wall for lack of a plot to base the story upon. This head-banging activity is not the least bit pleasurable although, as somebody said, it does feel good when you stop. People's lives generally consist of a series of digressions—not plots. You are born, you digress, and you die. Maybe then you're born again. Who knows? Maybe you're just laid to rest in a plot.

But plots are a contrivance that our artistic natures create in order to superimpose a meaningful structure upon our lives. They have no basis in fact whatsoever—they are sheer fiction.

Perhaps an animal's existence has a plot. I don't pretend to know one way or the other about that. What I do know, what I suspect anyway, is that a human being who determines to plot out his own life either dies too soon to appreciate the folly of such an ambition or lives long enough to suffer the tragic and disappointing consequences of it.

My life so far, seems to have been a random journey without any sense of destination. This has long been a cause of great anxiety for me. At times I would try to console myself with the thought that I was, perhaps, what is referred to as a 'late bloomer.' Of late, however, I am beginning to suspect that I shall end up rather bloomless and bloom-free, so to speak. There is solace to be had, however, in the fact that nearly everybody I've ever met suffers from the same sort of anxiety with regard to the capricious nature of their lives. It's stressful enough dealing with this situation on my own. If I was stressed and thought most other people were not stressed, then I'd be even more stressed, but knowing that nearly everybody is stressed and, perhaps, most of them being more stressed than me makes me feel less stressed, and I like that—if you get my drift.

It would be utterly unbearable if I thought other people weren't as equally frustrated with the whole ordeal as I am. I mean, it would be like finding out that death and taxes actually *don't* apply to everyone. Well okay, as we all know, some people don't pay taxes but that's because they are either so damn poor and disconnected that no government gives a hoot about them, or they are so damn rich they can afford clever lawyers to exempt them.

Nevertheless, no lawyer is clever enough to exempt anyone from eventual death. It would be the ultimate slap in the face to realize that some people are going to live healthy lives forever and ever while the rest of us must die. Those people would be an absolute pain in the ass to deal with. They could be as annoying as they wanted to be, and when it became evident that your tolerance was exhausted they'd merely smirk and say, "Hey, if you don't like it, shoot me . . . ha, ha."

No . . . I say, thank God for death. It's the great equalizer.

For most of my life I was under the false assumption that the vast assortment of experiences and knowledge I have been accumulating not only served to distinguish me in a favorable light compared to my peers, but would eventually earn me a certain ultimate position of place beyond them. This sort of thinking, of course, is utter silliness. We're all going to end up dead and forgotten regardless of our accomplishments—except for Elvis, that is. Still, I keep pushing the damn rock up the hill.

Each one of us is born with a finite allotment of breaths, heartbeats, and tears. The allotment varies from person to person. That is our fate. How ably we manage to conserve them has a great deal to do with determining our destiny.

Weary of searching for my destiny. . . . Let it find me!

Of course, as I consider the way I've lived my life, that's pretty much how I've always felt. Problem is, it hasn't found me yet. Then again, maybe that's not so bad. After all, it seems to me that what's important in life is not what happens *to* you; what's important is what happens *within* you.

Destiny has a habit of finding us all, one way or another, sooner or later. Last month, for example, I was up in Vientiane, the capital of Laos. I'd never been there before. On my first evening in town, I was at a riverside restaurant sitting in a plastic chair beside a plastic table. Wish I could say that I was sitting in a bamboo chair beside a bamboo table, but that would be a lie. Plastic has, for better or worse, supplanted so many of the artifacts and so much of the charm once associated with this part of the world that so enamored some of us from another part of the world. The legs of the table and chair were positioned snugly within the sandy shore of the mighty Mekong. I was drinking a lukewarm bottle of Beer Lao when I happened to strike up a conversation with a Kiwi fellow who had recently celebrated his own fiftieth birthday.

Vientiane is situated on the northern bank where the revered waterway flows tranquilly from west to east before turning the bend at the Thai town of Nong Khai to resume its southerly cruise towards . . . towards . . . well, look at a map for Christsakes . . . Cambodia, Vietnam, the South China Sea. Must I explain everything?

Legions of poor bedraggled children, their tender flesh encrusted with soil and sweat, scantily clad in filthy rags, offset with bellies bloated by malnutrition, beg for pennies from Beer Lao-sodden tourists such as myself who, more often than not, casually wave them away. Afterwards, we return to our pampered and affluent environs with soulful anecdotes hoping to impress family and friends with a phony pathos.

Actually, that is a rather harsh indictment—harsh and, in many cases, unfair. A true sense of pathos does not belong exclusively to the poor and destitute of this world . . . no more than malnourished souls belong to the materially pampered and affluent. Suffering and joy are everywhere. These are not commodities that can be bought and sold. Peace of mind doesn't sit on a shelf in a market place with a price tag around its neck. You can't buy it— you have to earn it. In truth, there is nothing really worth having in this world that can be bought or sold. Of course, I speak as one of the pampered and affluent for whom food, shelter, and clothing have always been affordable.

A polio crippled young man named Noi spends his evenings slithering through the sand—a beggar. He says he has no family, no home. He drags his withered limbs across the terraced restaurants begging for coins with nothing to offer but a beautiful smile and sparkling brown eyes. Just by way of keeping a bit of conversation going, I asked him what he wanted out of life. He said, "Vegetables and rice."

Oh well, I'd better stop with this line of narrative before I move myself to tears. Let's get back to the Kiwi. . . .

"My name's Joe, but people call me J for short," he declared.

"J-A-Y?" I asked.

"No, just J, he said. "J-A-Y wouldn't exactly be short for my name, would it?"

"No, I guess not. J-A-Y would be the same length as J-O-E."

"I don't spell my name J-O-E. I spell it J-O . . . Jo."

"I see." Funny that it was easier to get the beggar to explain what he wanted out of life than it was to get this guy to explain what the hell his name was.

"So, if people called me J-A-Y that would, in fact, be *long* for my name, right?"

"Right," I conceded. "But J and J-A-Y sound the same, don't they?"

"Not exactly. J sounds short and sharp. Sort of like me."

"J-A-Y sounds longer to you?"

"Oh, for sure."

Like I said, this Kiwi, J, had recently celebrated his fiftieth birthday—a year and a half earlier, to be precise—but I think by the time a person reaches fifty, anything that happened within three or four years is considered recent history. I asked him if turning fifty was an especially significant occasion for him, and he said,

"Yes. It was the first time in my life when I finally developed a passion for something."

As a prologue to this momentous event, J explained that he had had a rather lonely and lackluster childhood. His father died when he was a very young boy. (When J was a very young boy, that is.) He had no brothers.

"I lived with my mother, two older sisters, and an aunt," he said. "That's like being surrounded with too much treble and not enough bass, if you know what I mean."

I did.

"It took me five years to get through high school," he continued. "I wasn't a very good student, but then I had a business and otherwise I mostly played rugby."

"What kind of business did you have?" I asked.

"I mowed lawns."

"Ah, a landscaping business."

""Nope," he said. "I just mowed lawns. Cut a lot of grass . . . that was all. After high school I had many different jobs. None I much cared for, but I saved a fair bit of money. I bought a big old bus, fixed it up real luxurious like, and started a party bus business. Took people around the town for a night. They loved it. The business grew, I bought more buses, and branched out doing crosscountry trips. This went on for 18 years. Had some fun at it mind you, but basically it was just a job. Sold the business for quite a bit of money and went fishing for a few years. When that got boring I decided to take a vacation to Thailand. Sort of took a fancy to *Northern* Thailand and have been here nearly four years now."

"And on your fiftieth birthday you fell in love with a sweet little Thai woman . . . is that it?"

"No . . . an elephant."

"Oh, a sweet, *large* Thai woman," I said.

"No, I fell in love, so to speak, with an elephant."

"An elephant elephant?"

"A sweet Thai elephant, yes."

"Large animal with a long nose?"

"Right."

"Four footed mammal, thick hide, eats a lot?"

"That's the one," he said.

"What and how much were you drinking that night, J?"

"Ha! Now, now . . . it wasn't like that. I'd just developed a bit of a fascination with elephants when I came to Thailand. They're such majestic creatures. So powerful and yet so gentle. I read about them, visited the sites around here where they're trained and worked. I got to know some of their handlers, the mahouts. The more I learned about them, the more fascinated I became. Do you realize how much healthy adult elephants eat per day?"

"Well, judging from their size, my guess would be that they eat, approximately, one hell of a lot."

"Two to three hundred kilos of jungle foliage a day. Plus a hundred liters of water."

"Wow. Hard to imagine there's enough time in a day to consume all that."

"Your typical elephant spends about twenty hours a day feeding,"

"Really. How's he kill the rest of his time?"

"Chasing cow elephants and sleeping."

"What happens when he catches a cow elephant?"

"Then they have sex, but that only lasts about twenty seconds. The chase takes a lot longer. Male elephants are not especially skilled at foreplay."

"Not much for oral sex, huh?"

"Oh no, fellatio and cunnilingus are not part of an elephant's bag of tricks."

"And after this twenty-second orgy of lust, I suppose they're back munching away at the forest again."

"Yeah, pretty much so. But, of course, they do rest once in a while."

"So let me get this straight," I said. "Your average, run-of-the-mill elephant's daily routine consists of eating the jungle for twenty hours, having sex for twenty seconds, and taking a short nap every so often. Is that about right?"

"That pretty much sums up their day, right. I mean, let's be honest, they don't lead a particularly enviable existence. Being born an elephant probably isn't at the top of one's list for a future reincarnation."

"No, I shouldn't think so. Still, they seem to be essentially peaceful creatures, so I suppose that's got to count for something."

"That's very true. Elephants are extremely peaceful creatures. They don't prey on any other animals and, in fact, their only serious predator is Man."

"Wouldn't you know it? God blasted humans! Anyway, I suppose it's fair to say that unless you're a vegetable you wouldn't have much to fear from elephants."

"Well, you wouldn't want to be a banana or a stick of sugarcane, either."

"Oh, right."

"And cow elephants will attack if their young are threatened."

"I've always made it a rule in my life never to threaten young elephants."

"Good policy."

I told J that I was approaching the fiftieth commemoration of my birthday and, without hesitation, he offered to buy me another big bottle of Beer Lao. Feigning a mock hesitation at accepting the offer, I made a mental note that this might be an effective ploy to cadge free drinks on future occasions. While gazing pleasantly upon a sampan fisherman plying his trade in the middle of the Mekong—which meant he was technically right on the border of Thailand and Laos—I accepted the offer. Mind you, I did so graciously, which is important to do. When the beer arrived, I proceeded to query my Kiwi benefactor further about his "passion." *Quid pro quo*, as the Romans used to say.

"So, elephants, as you said, have become your passion."

"Yes. You like this beer?" he asked.

"Beer Lao?"

"Yes."

"Sure. It could be colder but, otherwise, I like it."

You bet . . . a free bottle of lukewarm Beer Lao served up at a plastic table on a sandy bank of the Mekong beat the hell out of a bottle of Dom Perignon in a sterling silver ice bucket at Maxim's Bar in Paris that I couldn't afford. "Say a Prayer for Me Tonight," as the song goes.

"What is it about elephants that most concerns you?" I asked.

"Their teeth."

"Their teeth?"

"Yes. I've been working in consultation with several dentists—two in Thailand and a particular friend of mine back in New Zealand. Thailand is quite well known for the high quality of its dental profession, you know."

"I didn't know that, actually. I do, however, know that the country has perhaps the finest micro-surgeons in the world with regard to a specific type of operation. Namely, the re-attachment of severed penises."

"Well now," said J, "I did not know that."

"Oh yes. If for no other reason than they get plenty of practice around here."

"Do they, indeed?"

"It's a fairly common practice for a Thai woman to cut off her husband's penis if he drunkenly abuses her too often, or she finds out he's fooling around with other women."

"It's a fairly common practice for Thai men to drink too much and whore around with other women."

"Exactly. As I suppose it is for men of all nationalities. Here, unfortunately, they run the risk of having their pride and joy fed to the chickens."

"How do you mean?"

"It's called 'feeding the chickens.' The woman will get up early while her husband's still unconscious from a night of drunken debauchery, grab a kitchen knife, slice off his penis, and toss it into the backyard where the chickens are. I lived for five years on Koh Samui surrounded by these busybody, pick-pecking, flightless birds. Believe me, chickens will eat just about anything."

"That's interesting. I should hope that it will never become useful information but, the more I live here the more I realize that Thais have a bit of a violent streak in their nature."

"Oh, more than just a bit, I'd say."

"Certainly more than the tourist brochures indicate."

"Considerably more than that, yes."

"And yet, the elephant, which is one of the country's national symbols—like the bald eagle is to America—is such a gentle, non-violent creature. It's their patron saint of animals, so to speak. Elephants are often abused here, of course, but at the same time, they're highly revered."

"Thailand is nothing if not a country of rampant and curious contradictions. I'm loath to say that they're part of her charm, but they certainly have a great deal to do with the exotic mystique."

"It's a pity that aside from revering the elephant—which I honestly believe they do for all the right reasons—they don't also learn more from its example."

"As you have?"

"I've been trying," he said.

"So tell me how it is that you came to be concerned with their teeth. It never occurred to me that elephants, you know . . ."

"Have a need for dental care?"

"Yes. That's what never occurred to me," I said.

"Well, it's like this. An elephant grows six sets of teeth during the course of its life. Every ten years or so, one set of teeth falls out and another set grows in."

"Okay."

"But when the sixth set falls out, that's it—no more teeth. An elephant without teeth can't eat. Consequently, most elephants die of starvation around the age of seventy."

"Not a pleasant way to die."

"No. So, what I've been working on is a way to manufacture and supply elephants with dentures. With a properly designed and workable set of dentures, elephants could live for another twenty to thirty years."

J continued to talk further for 15 minutes or so about elephants, and I continued to listen. It wasn't so much the subject that interested me, as it was the man's passion for it. I would never have thought that listening about the plight of these creatures would hold my genuine attention for as long as it did.

There is, no doubt, a certain contagious buoyancy with regard to any subject that one man with a passion for can arouse in another man. I don't think it makes much difference what that subject may be. What occurred to me was what a thrill it has always been to be in the company of people who have been in the company of a passion for something or someone other than merely transient and tawdry desires. The world is crawling with passionless souls.

I, at times, think myself to be one of them. It was heartening for me to realize that J didn't find his until he was fifty.

Hope springs eternal.

———

Two weeks ago it was my father's birthday. He's been dead for a long time now, but I still think about him. . . .

When my father was a young man, he dreamed that one day he would own a small manufacturing company. When I was a young man, I dreamed of moving to Paris and living the expat, bohemian life of a bygone era. . . .

My father was a Navy pilot during World War II and graduated with an engineering degree from the Illinois Institute of Technology. He married, sired five children, and worked his entire career for rather large corporations. I married, sired nothing, had the arrangement annulled after three years, and ended up working for him shortly thereafter. It was at a small manufacturing company on the Northwest side of Chicago. A small manufacturing company just like he had wanted. It was involved in the precision machining of plastics and metals—supplying various bits and pieces of this and that to very large aerospace, electronic, and medical research firms.

My university degree in philosophy had prepared me for nothing, and so I had failed at everything. All I wanted was to go to Paris, smoke Gauloises, drink café au lait all day, cheap wine all night, and . . . and pretend I was part of the 'Lost Generation' that had long since passed away. In our different fashions, I suspect my father and I just wanted to be left alone. As it turned out, at least for a while, we got stuck with one another at this damn little job-shop called Jetron.

He had bought the company with two other business partners. One of them made an appearance at the end of every month to pick up a check. The other one never came by at all. Had to fork out postage for his monthly return on investment. That suited my father just fine. He ran the joint.

My youngest brother, the baby of the family, had been working at Jetron for two years before I showed up on the scene. By that time he was assistant sales manager—learning the ropes, as the saying goes—and doing quite well. They hired me on an interim basis to do whatever was needed to be done that didn't require any skills, and the only ropes I was learning were those that I needed to avoid so as not to hang myself. Basically, I was just there to help out where I could, and make enough money to cover my expenses for the trip to Paris. My father knew that. In fact, I had told him. He always seemed to have a bit of trouble making heads or tails out of me, but I always knew he loved me. I could exasperate the hell out of him; still he loved me.

Anyway, by the beginning of September 1979 I was one month away from heading for Paris. Already had the ticket. Went to the bank with my father ten o'clock on a Wednesday morning. It was a big, big day for him. We sat at a conference table and passed documents and certified checks around. He paid off his two partners. By eleven o'clock the manufacturing company was his. Mind you, he owed the bank a crap load of money but, nevertheless, my father finally had his dream.

I said let's go have lunch, get drunk, and celebrate. Any excuse not to go back to work, I figured, was a good one. He said not today son, got to go downtown to Northwestern Memorial for a check-up. He checked in, had his check-up, and checked out three weeks later. Buried him a couple of days before my dream flight to Paris. Poor bastard never set foot in Jetron after it was all his, and I never set foot on that plane.

Funny thing about my father dying . . . our dreams got sort of switched around. He got the big flight out of town and I got stuck managing the damn little manufacturing company. Not that either one of us wanted it that way. All the time he lay dying in the hospital bed, he never once put any pressure on me to stick around. Never invited me to participate in any meetings with my brother and the lawyer about how the company should be set up and managed. He just took it for granted that I would walk away from the whole mess.

Then, late on the afternoon before he died, I visited him. Only the two of us in the room. A room full of pukey green colors and the stench of death. I'd just come back from running all around the North Side of Chicago trying to find him a goddamn banana Popsicle. That's what he wanted. His throat was so dried out he could hardly swallow, and he asked for a banana Popsicle. Had to be banana. Just like a little kid. Took me two hours to find one, but it was worth it. He was so pleased when I returned with it. Probably a test or something. Wanted to see if I had it in me to find exactly what he had asked for. Like a damn scavenger hunt or something.

So, he was lying there dying and sucking on this damn banana Popsicle and I told him I wasn't going to Paris. Said I figured I better stick around and help out with the company. He said forget it, the company didn't need my help. I said tough shit, I'm sticking around anyway. He said oh yeah? Well, you want to stick around, there's only one job for you. Every successful organization needs a son of a bitch. You want to be the son of a bitch, he said, okay you can stick around. Otherwise, no deal.

So, that was the deal. Fifteen long years I stuck around as the resident son of a bitch. Got pretty damn good at it, too. Nobody really liked me much, but the company did pretty well for a few years. Paid off the debts and actually made some decent money. 'Course, my kid-brother was the president and we wouldn't have made shit if he hadn't been such a good salesman and all. If you put that to him, he'd probably deny it. My brother is a humble soul. Got to respect a fellow like that, and everybody who knows him does. Some people are given credit for being humble when, in fact, they're merely insecure. Genuine humility requires a great deal of self-confidence. No doubt that's one reason he was such a good salesman. But, the ol' man was right. Got to have a son of a bitch. Fire people, kick ass . . . that sort of stuff.

Anyway, 15 years of that malarkey and I retired to an island in the Gulf of Siam. 'Bout as far away from my father's dream as one could possibly get. No company, no family, no responsibilities . . . I loved it! Sat on that island for five years and did pretty much nothing. Yep, loved every minute of it.

For the past two years I've been all over the map. Thailand, Cambodia, Morocco, France, Greece. Now I'm in Bangkok and thinking, once again, maybe it's time for Paris. However, my declining financial affairs have made it quite plain to me that moving to Paris at this time is not a viable option. In fact, moving anywhere is pretty much out of the question.

So, I got myself a nice little one-bedroom apartment on the twenty-eighth floor of a joint called Omni Towers. Fully furnished and barely affordable. Bangkok at my feet. Bangkok stuck to my feet. Six hundred feet up in a concrete tree-house overlooking this metropolitan jungle of Bangkok. I'm on the east side of the building. The rising sun side. The side where all the Japanese live. The west side overlooks the swimming pool. That's the side the Westerners prefer. I think the Japs know better.

It's the beginning of March. The hot season is about to commence and I wouldn't want that damn blazing sun glaring into my apartment all afternoon. Still, it is somewhat comforting to have a place to call home again. Never in my wildest dreams did I ever think Bangkok would be that place, but so it is. Now, instead of being all over the map, I'm all over one street. A street called Soi Nana. . . .

The north end of Soi Nana butts up against Sukhumvit Road, which is one of the main thoroughfares of Bangkok and, if I remember reading correctly, the longest-running road in Thailand. At this end of the *soi*, a petrol station is on the west side and a cement and glassed-in police bunker is on the east side. This bunker construction seems to have been strategically placed so as to provide optimum nuisance for the poor, hapless pedestrians who ply the sidewalks around the neighborhood.

Bangkok is clearly one of the most pedestrian-unfriendly cities in the world. Motorcycle taxis regularly whiz along the sidewalk. Even policemen on motorcycles drive through pedestrians. I confronted one of them about that last week and was duly informed, "Bangkok policeman do what he want, you understand?" This gentleman's command of the English language indicated that he was obviously a member of the provident Tourist Police brigade. Frankly, I hadn't realized up to then that Bangkok police were entitled to do whatever they wanted to. Silly of me, of course. Useful information to keep in mind.

The gentlemen inside the bunker are traffic police and, as far as I can determine, it is their job to oversee the usually chaotic ebb and flow of toxic-fume-emitting vehicles that clutter the intersection. 'Oversee' is the operative and only verb one could reasonably associate with their behavior. The bunker is what you might call an observation post. It looks like a fairly comfortable, air-conditioned abode from which to view the chaos. Nothing ever seems be done to alleviate it.

Immediately behind the bunker is a middle-aged Thai man who sits all day and long into the evening hunched over on a wooden stool. He's a combination cobbler and key grinder. When he's not nailing new heels onto soles of shoes, he's shooting sparks from his grinding wheel. When he's not engaged in either one of those occupations he simply sits hunched over, looking the picture of unkempt idleness. Guy ought to sit up straight once in a while or he's going to ruin his back.

Across a narrow, broken stretch of pavement from the cobbler-key grinder is an open-air shop that sells luggage. In front of this shop is a man hawking the services of a nearby massage parlor. "Nice girls, good service," he says. Heading south is Tom's Qwik hamburger joint, a photography and photocopy shop, newspaper stall, fried food stalls, and the first of a couple hundred beer bars that are Soi Nana's main attraction. Men of all ages, shapes and sizes, and varying degrees of wealth and intelligence seem to find common ground when it comes to drinking booze and ogling and fondling young, attractive women in various stages of undress. Why is that. . . ? Hard to imagine my father being one of them. But, if there's any truth to the expression 'like father, like son' he would have been, had he ever the opportunity.

Sometimes, early on a Saturday or Sunday morning, I'll stand at the window of my twenty-eighth-floor apartment, and as my drowsy eyes lazily scan the concrete jungle of Bangkok, it seems completely lifeless. Not a sound to be heard; not a movement to be seen. But, if I open the window I can hear the birds singing. And then silently, like a snake in the grass, an elevated train glides along its rails weaving through the sprawl of mortar below me.

So it was this Saturday morning. I woke up all alone and fifty years old. According to my trusty little bedside alarm clock it was 6:27 a.m. The sun had just crept above the roof of the Grand Pacific Hotel. As I said, the Japanese live on the east side of the building and all the white folks live on the west side overlooking the swimming pool. Not sure why that is. Probably due to some juxtaposition of cultural anomalies with which I am not familiar. Japan—Land of the Rising Sun. The West—land of the horny white guys with binoculars. Who knows? The rising sun suits me fine.

This morning, as I often do, I turned on my computer for a few games of hearts. Pauline, Michele, Ben, and McFinn. In essence, it's me against the three of them. They team up against me every stinking chance they get. Nevertheless, I still manage to win most of the time. Hearts is my game. I'm good at hearts. Hearts is a card game to me. Only hearts I've had anything to do with in years. 'Shoot the moon' every chance I get. I'm a reckless and aggressive player of the game. Playing not to get any hearts bores me. I want 'em all and that black bitch of spades as well. Sometimes I get all but one. That's when I know that Pauline and Michele and Ben are conspiring against me. They hate it when I gloat after kicking their butts for a few games. So, they set me up. Give me a near perfect hand to go for the moon and then, at the last minute, one of them screws me. That's all right. It prepares me to face the day. Cruel world and all that.

Next I check my e-mail. Nine times out of ten there isn't any. See, nobody cares about me. That's what I mean—only hearts I deal with are fucking video cards!

With all this excitement out of the way, I did nothing of note for the rest of the day other than to loll around anticipating my evening at the Bamboo Bar. . . .

———

I arrived at the hotel a little before nine o'clock. A fancily dressed doorman opened the taxi door, and another one opened the door leading into the lobby. A sign indicated that tonight the Bamboo Bar would be the venue for a series of brief readings from a play called *The Rock Bottom Good-bye* written by a woman named Genevieve

AT THE BAMBOO BAR

Langdon. That seemed unusual I thought, but as long as it didn't interrupt the flow of booze, they'd get no objection from me.

I went straight to the bar and took a stool along the rail. Well all right, I didn't actually take the stool, I sat on it. Right in the middle of the bar. Behind me and off to the left at the corner table in front of the windows along the outside passageway sat an elderly woman in a wheelchair. She was all alone with an aperitif glass of amber fluid and not looking the least bit lonely.

Two weeks earlier I had gone to the Bamboo Bar in the middle of an afternoon just to scope the joint out. Get the lay of the land, so to speak. There was nobody in the place except the bartender. His name is Sompong. I nursed a couple of very pricey draft beers and asked a few cheap questions. Sompong did his best to humor me while he went about setting up the bar for the evening's traffic.

I asked him to tell me some interesting stories about the place.

"The King and Queen came in one night unannounced," he said. "They were on their way to Sydney for the Olympics. The place was packed, no tables available. The doorman was in a panic but he saw a couple at a table in the back that appeared to be ready to leave. He very tactfully expedited their departure. The royal couple, dressed casually, entered discreetly, sat down, and ordered drinks. Queen, a gin and tonic; King, I forget. Only four security guards stationed around the room.

"King Juan Carlos of Spain did more or less the same, except he came in just before 3:00 a.m. when the bar was getting ready to close. Needless to say, he got a drink."

Sompong then proceeded to rattle off more names of various celebrities who have visited the bar. Elton John, Gore Vidal, Oliver Stone, etcetera.

I said I wasn't interested in celebrities—they nauseate me.

His fist tightened around a bar rag and he looked at me menacingly.

"Not the King and Queen of Thailand, of course," I hastened to add. "They're wonderful! Long live the King, I say. He's the greatest!" And he is. "Pity he doesn't have more control of affairs."

"That's the truth," said Sompong.

"It's the ho-hum celebrities you mention that nauseate me."

"Oh," he said. "Well, to tell you the truth, most of them are spoiled brats. They nauseate me, as well. It's disgusting what qualifies for celebrity these days."

"Tell me some funny incidents," I said.

"Okay," said Sompong. "A guy came in with his wife and another couple, drank champagne for five hours until there wasn't any more of that particular champagne left." When the guy ordered another bottle, Sompong says sorry, all we got left is Dom Perignon. Guy says fine, bring us a bottle of that stuff. Sompong's thinking DP is three times the cost of what they'd been drinking so he says to the guy, you want to know how much it is? Guy says hey, you insult me asking that kind of question and embarrass me in front of my friends. So, Sompong apologizes and brings over the DP. When the guy gets ready to leave and sees the bill, he says oh my Buddha! How come you didn't tell me how much this DP stuff costs? Then he starts laughing. "Just joking with me," said Sompong.

I asked Sompong if he tells jokes to the customers? American bartenders tell jokes.

Sompong said no, he doesn't tell jokes. Too risky. So many different nationalities—not sure who's going to find one joke funny and another joke that makes no sense.

I said well, here's a good simple joke for you. It's my favorite joke of all time. Might even consider it a Thai joke, but it isn't really. You want to hear it. . . ? Yeah. Okay, here goes. . . . Why did the monkey fall out of the tree? I paused for a moment just to get the timing right, and Sompong repeated, "Why did the monkey fall out of the tree?" Perfect audience! And I said, "'Cause it was dead."

He loved it . . . said he was going try it out sometime.

I told him that I worked on and off for six years in restaurants and bars—busboy, waiter, assistant cook, bartender, and doorman, etcetera. In America, people often sit at a bar and tell their problems to the bartender. I asked Sompong if that happens to him. He said it doesn't because, first of all, most of the patrons speak English— "My English is not so good . . . especially when people start to tell me about their troubles, if you know what I mean"—and, second of all, people who can afford to drink at the Bamboo Bar probably don't got any real problems worth talking about anyway. I thought to myself, that's highly unlikely, but it's a conviction based less upon a cultural and more of a personal philosophical bias. Yes, I know, an anomaly if there ever was one . . . which I'm not going to elaborate upon. Think East versus West. Otherwise, you either get it or you don't.

Sompong worked the trade in New York City for a number of years. He speaks English very well, despite his own modest opinion. I asked him if he'd ever heard of the American writer F. Scott Fitzgerald. He hadn't. Fitzgerald, I told him, once wrote that the only difference between rich people and poor people is that rich people have more money. Sompong laughed and then said there was more to it than that. He grew up in a poor neighborhood. Another difference between poor people and rich people, he said, is that rich people are much more demanding.

I paid my tab, told Sompong I'd be back for my birthday, and casually walked around the room before I left. . . . Persian carpets on teakwood floors, walls and ceiling hand painted by two women artists from Hong Kong. Hand painted, said Sompong—as in they didn't use brushes. The peach-colored paint was literally applied by hand and a special type of sponge. You have to look closely to realize it. Clearly, when it comes to the exhibition of a refined artistry of ambient style, the Thais are second to none in Asia.

———

Generally, I prefer to sit at the end of a bar. The Bamboo Bar is in the shape of an elongated 'S' and only has about ten stools against it. At one end, in front of the band stage, was a guy sitting by himself drinking whiskey colas. Never met anyone in my life that mixed booze with cola that I wanted to spend much time talking to, and I was in no mood to make an exception on the occasion of my fiftieth birthday. I strolled down to the other end of the bar where I'd never sat before. The stool was unoccupied. Just as I was on the verge of altering that status, a pretty girl in traditional Thai garb informed me that permission to sit on that particular stool would not be forthcoming .

"This is the service area," she said.

"Good. That's what I'm here for," I said. "So, serve me."

"Service area for waitress, not customer," she said.

Too bad for me. The bar was crowded. Seems everywhere I turn these days, I am confronted by overpopulation. Every time I turn around, there it is—overpopulation. Over here, over there . . . overpopulation is all over everywhere. If only people would all chip in, we could help solve this problem. It wouldn't take much— little effort, little expense. Buy a bullet, borrow a gun . . . shoot yourself. Or, shoot a friend. Have a friend shoot you, whatever. Suicide and murder. Just the thought of it compels my eyebrows to raise themselves.

I was invited to sit at the one other empty stool midway along the bar; the one I'd just left. Why there's a stool in front of the service area remains a mystery. But then again, Bangkok is a mysterious place, and I suppose that's part of its charm.

So down I sat. On my left was a sixtyish-year-old gentleman in a short-sleeved, pink silk shirt and black cotton pants hunched over the financial pages of the *Herald Tribune*. He was drinking a see-through of some sort. Maybe gin, maybe vodka. Not sure. To my right was an English couple on holiday. They were drinking champagne. I ordered an Irish whiskey on the rocks. My fiftieth birthday celebration was underway. . . . Man, that whiskey tasted good. Put me in a pleasant, convivial mood with the first sip.

I turned my head left and said, "So, how are things in the real world?"

"Bloody awful if you don't mind," replied the pink silk shirt. He didn't even look at me.

"Sorry to hear that," I said. "Modesty Blaise was looking fine and sexy in today's *Bangkok Post*. Maybe you should check out the comics' page. She's a sight for sore eyes if you want my opinion."

This time he looked at me but didn't say anything. The expression on his face, however, suggested that he wasn't the least bit interested in my opinion about Modesty Blaise or anything else, and that my spirit of conviviality was a damn nuisance as far as he was concerned. I got the message. Ornery bastard!

It would take more than that to spoil my party, though.

I had noticed a Bangkok guidebook positioned between the glasses of champagne in front of the English couple. That's the reason I figured they were here as tourists. Fifty years old and my mind is still pretty sharp. They weren't saying much to each other; married I supposed. So, I said, "You folks finding your way around Bangkok all right?" I nodded at the guidebook as I said this in order to rationalize the query. It wouldn't seem proper to accost a couple of absolute strangers with a question that didn't make any sense. After all, the Bamboo Bar is a pretty classy place and, of course, English people have to be treated with a certain degree of deference or they'll think you're undermining their respectability.

And, if there is one thing English people will not tolerate being undermined, it's their respectability. They established and maintained an empire based upon it for Christsakes!

The female member of the partnership replied, "Oh indeed, we've been managing quite well so far, thank you. It's a much lovelier city than we'd expected. Isn't that right, Charles?"

Charles maneuvered an eyebrow in a fashion I interpreted as a sign of agreement, and the woman continued: "My husband and I have been here nearly a week, and if I do say so myself, I think we've sorted ourselves out quite nicely thus far. The people are simply adorable. So gracious and friendly . . . wouldn't you say, Charles?"

Charles worked the eyebrow again while taking a sip of effervescence in the process.

"You're from the States, aren't you?" she said to me. "I could tell from your accent. My friends say I'm quite clever at picking out peoples' nationalities based on the way they speak. I fancy you're from . . . let me see . . . oh, let's say the New England states somewhere. Is that correct?"

I paused for a moment because I wasn't sure if she had just asked a question that was meant to be answered.

"Well. . . ?" she persisted.

Charles raised both his eyebrows, asked for the check and, just to prove that he was capable of human speech, said, "Darling, we'll be late for dinner if we don't get a move on."

"Pleasure talking to you, young man," she said to me. And off they went.

"Chicago," I said to my Irish whiskey.

Young man, uh? Fifty years old and she calls me a young man. See, people are living longer. No question about it.

What's a guy supposed to be thinking about on his fiftieth birthday? His life? What he's done with it? Accomplishments? The people I know from Chicago tell me that the thing they are most proud of is their family—their children, especially.

Everybody is proud of their children.

"It's not the mere fact of having children that I take pride in," explained an old high school classmate of mine. "Any jackass can sire a litter. That doesn't require much talent. The challenge comes in raising the children properly."

"Properly?" I asked.

"Yes."

"What's properly?"

"Properly means that you raise a child to know the difference between right and wrong, to respect other people, and to become a productive, law-abiding member of society."

This guy was a senior when I was a freshman. He'd been assigned to me as a sort of mentor-guardian. A 'big brother' so to speak. They did that kind of thing where I went to high school. It was a Jesuit prep school called Campion on the banks of the Mississippi River in the godforsaken town of Prairie du Chien, Wisconsin. My father went there. He loved it. Said the four years he spent there were the best four years of his life. I hated the joint and figured if those four years were going to be the best four years of my life, I mind as well shoot myself and get it over with.

My 'big-brother' was an 'A' class student, captain of the varsity wrestling team, vice-president of the student body government, member of the forensics club, and one of the top officers of ROTC. I can't even remember what ROTC stands for. It's a student military organization of some sort. Twice a week we all got dressed up in drab-green uniforms and marched around the quadrangle like a bunch of toy soldiers.

You might say Campion was a semi-military institution. In fact, it was basically a glorified reform school for recalcitrant adolescent males who had already exhibited tell-tale signs of not growing up to be productive, law-abiding citizens. Many of my classmates were not the budding progeny that a man celebrating his fiftieth birthday was going to consider one of his life's proud accomplishments.

The poor sucker who got stuck being my 'big-brother' happened to be passing through Bangkok on a business trip two years ago. It was a complete accident that we met here. Fortunately it was the kind of accident you could walk away from afterwards. Maybe a couple of ego bruises but no physical damage. He was staying at the Sheraton Grande Hotel, a very nice five-star encampment on Sukhumvit Road. I often hang out there whenever I'm in town. Great buffet, world-class gym and sauna, a marvelous swimming pool in a garden setting, and a very gracious staff.

Many members of this very gracious staff know me by name. I like that. They call me Khun Mac. And they *wai* me. A *wai* is the charming Thai custom of greeting someone by pressing the palms of your hands together while bowing your head slightly. It's a comfort to know that whenever I'm feeling a bit down on my luck, I can always go over to the Sheraton Grande and be greeted by name with a smile and a bow. Some days I'll hang out there for hours.

On the particular day that I ran into my Campion big-brother, I was helping myself to a second serving of sushi at the Orchid Café buffet. I heard the sweet, tingling bells on the hand-held message board being paraded around the room by one of the hotel pageboys. Someone was wanted on the phone. I've never been paged for a phone call in my life. Still, I always glance at the board expectantly. Maybe it's the bells; maybe it's an ego thing. Who cares?

Naturally, being in Bangkok, the name on the board is often written in some Asian script that I can't read, let alone pronounce. That rules me out right from the start. Other times it will be a French or German name, but that's getting closer to me. Whenever it's an Anglo-Saxon name, I actually perk up just a bit. Of course, it's never me, but sometimes I'm tempted to take the call anyway. Just to be on the stage for a moment you understand.

"Mr. Howard Kalb." That was the name on the board.

A fellow two tables away from me signaled to the pageboy. I recognized him immediately. Short cropped, light brown hair; medium height; broad shoulders; and all dressed up in a tan cotton suit, white shirt, and a red paisley tie. Howie Kalb, no question about it. He was sitting with a couple of Thai gentlemen.

I went to meet him in the lobby on his way back from the phone call. We were both thrilled with the chance encounter and arranged to get together for drinks that evening. Seems Campion grads are always thrilled to see one another regardless of how tenuous the friendship may have been while they were at school together.

A certain sort of bonding occurs between boys who are sent away from home at a young age to fend for themselves in the relatively severe confines of a boarding school environment. No one ever says when they "graduated" from Campion. They tell you the year they "got out."

So, later that evening we met for drinks, and Howie talked about his kids, showed me the family photo he keeps in his wallet—all the usual stuff. Still, I was happy to see him. Sometime between the third and fourth Scotch, he gave air to the comment about raising children to become productive, law-abiding members of society.

Most of what he said sounded as if it had been memorized from a textbook.

I pointed out to him that I had, for all intents and purposes, removed myself from the society to which he referred, and was enjoying a rather purposeless existence in Thailand.

"Somehow that doesn't surprise me," he said.

"No?"

"No. I had a hunch after dealing with you during the first few months we knew each other at Campion that fitting into society wasn't going to be easy for you. In fact, I'm surprised the Jesuits didn't kick you out of the place."

"They did."

"Really?"

"Yeah, after the third year."

"What for?"

"'Bad attitude' was the way they put it."

"Hell, you had a bad attitude the moment you got off the train. You mean it took the Jebbies three years to figure that out?"

"No. You can say a lot of things about Jesuits, but I never met a dumb one. They knew I had a bad attitude all along. I think it just took them three years to figure out that it was beyond rehabilitation and they didn't want to tolerate it any longer."

"And now you're here."

"Yeah. The Thais are a lot more tolerable than Jesuits."

"Maybe that's because they don't have any strong principles to believe in."

"Sure they do. One of them is to leave people the fuck alone. There are no proselytizers over here."

"No proselytizers, just prostitutes, uh?"

"I guess I prefer the prostitutes."

"Well, to each his own, Mac."

"Now, that's mighty tolerable of you, Howie."

"You're not my responsibility. You want to screw around with prostitutes, that's your business."

"But, if I were your son or if one of the prostitutes was your daughter, then what?"

"That would never happen."

"How do you know?"

"Because like I said earlier, they were raised properly."

"Oh bullshit, Howie. You think I was raised improperly? You think Thai girls are raised to be prostitutes? What are you, nuts?"

"I think you've gotten it into your head that tolerance is a virtue."

"You mean it isn't?"

"Not categorically."

"There's one of those nice fat Jesuit words. 'Categorically.' Ha!"

"The tolerance of evil is not a virtue. That's my point, Mac."

"And a prostitute is evil? A man who has sex with a prostitute is evil?"

This guy was getting on my nerves. He was getting on my nerves that evening, and here I am letting him get on my nerves again. Why do I do that? This is my birthday for Christsakes, I thought. He used to get on my nerves 35 years ago. Forget about him. Dwell on pleasantries. Like prostitutes, for example. No, just kidding.

I ordered another Irish whiskey. Seven bucks a shot is what they charge for one of these babies in this joint. Most guys I went to school with wouldn't blink an eye at dropping seven bucks for a shot of booze. Woe is me, I guess. Well, not really. I'm happy being me. Being me has been a damn good gig for the most part. Who else would I want to be? Or could I be? Hell, I've enough trouble trying to be me, and that's after fifty years of practice. Too late in the game to try being somebody else. I mean sure, I wish I had more money. I wish I had as much money as so and so, but not if I had to *be* so and so. Just give me his money and let me carry on as myself.

Wish I could dance like Fred Astaire. Wish I could do anything like Fred Astaire. He's the closest thing to a hero I've ever had in my life. I'd be thrilled if I could just learn how to walk across the street like Fred Astaire. But, would I want to actually be Fred Astaire? No. No, absolutely not. Especially considering the fact that he's dead. No harm in emulating him, though.

One of my traits that I'm particularly grateful for is being able to appreciate greatness. Now, this is a pleasant subject to think about on my fiftieth birthday. Greatness. Fred Astaire, Muhammad Ali, the Beatles, and Johnny Carson—they were all great at what they did. In my estimation, they were each the greatest at their own chosen professions. Nope, no harm in appreciating and, even, emulating greatness. There should be more of that going around these days.

Probably my parents had something to do with developing this trait of mine. This penchant for appreciating greatness. There must have been something 'proper' about the way I was raised. Okay, so I play around with prostitutes once in a while. At least they're great-looking girls. You can take my word for that.

Another pair of tourists parked their carcasses on the stools recently vacated by the Brits, ordered two of those stupid-looking Polynesian concoctions with the paper umbrellas, and looked around the joint like a couple of bank robbers scoping out their next job.

"So *this* is the Bamboo Bar," said the blade of the species.

"Honestly dear, I thought there'd be more plants and stuff. Ferns and flowers and orchids and things. It's not as tropical as I expected. I mean, there's more foliage in these drinks than they've got around this room."

"Well that's the truth isn't it, honey-bun. Ought to serve these drinks with a machete for God's sake."

"Oh darling, you are funny."

"At least the bar is bamboo. Got to admit that much."

"This is marble or something, silly. It's not bamboo."

"No, not the surface of the bar, sugar-plum. Lookie here . . . along the edge. This here brown tube-like stuff is bamboo."

"You sure?"

"Sure as shootin'. That's bamboo or my name's not Willard C. Calhoun. Them damn Japs used to beat us boys pretty mean with it. Never forget. No ma'am, I recognizes bamboo when I sees it."

"I'm sorry, Will. I was really a hopin' this trip wouldn't be flarin' up them nasty days of yours."

"Two hunnurd and seventy-seven nasty days to be exact. But never you mind. Over and done with. We gonna have ourselves a good ol' time here in Thailand. Just you wait and see, sugar."

"Havin' a grand time already, dear. Just imagine, you and me, couple a' down-home folks from the coalfields of West Virginia sittin' purtty as can be at the world famous Bamboo Bar in the Oriental Hotel in Bangkok, Thailand. Number one hotel in the world, so's they say. Who'd a thought it!"

"Guess the Good Lord finally takin' a shine to us."

"I always put my faith in the Lord, dear."

"Yes 'um. And a bit of faith in that whippersnapper cousin a' yours. Fine boy, Bobby. Well schooled, too. Best darn stockbroker ever come out of our neck of the woods, I'd say. Sure do know how to pick 'em, don't he? Pick 'em and skin 'em, you might say."

"Bobby always was a bright boy. Even as a child that boy had a good head on his shoulders. And how about that dog of his."

"Oh my, yes! Saint Bernard it is. Only Saint Bernard in the entire state of West Virginia, fer as I know. Big as a pony. Got a bark like the sound of heavy furniture bein' moved across an oak wood floor. They use them kind of dogs to rescue people on the mountains of Switzerland, you know. Bobby likes to say that dog is the mascot of his business. Sure did rescue us financially."

"But still, like you said, the Lord was a watchin' over us."

"Praise the Lord. He's our salvation. Let's raise our glasses to 'im."

"To the Lord."

"To the Lord, to Bobby, and to Microsoft. Praise be to 'em all."

By this time I was beginning to think that the 'bank robbers' metaphor was slightly off the mark. Of course, they did sound like they may have had a bit of Bonnie and Clyde in them. More like Ma and Pa Kettle though, I reckon.

The gentleman in the pink silk shirt on my left, scanning through the *Herald Tribune*, ordered another drink. "Another gin and tonic, if you please," he said.

"You hear that man speak?" Will whispered to his wife. "Betcha he's an English bloke. Whaddya say?"

"Darlin', you're the world traveler. Don't suppose I'd recognize an Englishman if he were to trip over me."

"Just cuzz I hit a couple islands in the Pacific during the war don't make me no world traveler, sugar. Nevertheless, I did run in with a few of them English and Aussie fellers at the prison camp. Not real friendly at first. Especially them English boys. You gots to sort of wheedle your way into their good graces. But they can be mighty fine company once ya breaks through the outer crust."

"Well, I sure would like to meet me one of them. You think it would be all right if we said hello to him, Will?"

"Don't rightly see why not, sugar-plum. Ain't no harm in bein' friendly. He's all by his lonesome, too. Probably welcome a chance to chew the fat some. You go ahead. Just lean over and say hello."

I picked up my whiskey and leaned back slightly, clearing the way for her.

She smiled appreciatively at me and addressed Pinky: "Howdy, mister," she said. "My name's Betsy-May. Yer an Englishman, ain't ya? Never met a real Englishman. Be pleased to meet ya."

At the Bamboo Bar

Pinky looked at her with a perfectly blended visage of annoyance and condescension. Then, swallowing all that was left of his beverage, he droned, "I beg your pardon."

"By golly, you *are* an Englishman. I seen some English actors in the movies and they sound just like you. What luck! Will, did you hear that? Just like in the movies, ain't he?"

"Honestly, madam. If you please . . ."

"Oh, pardon us, mister," said Willard, joining the tableaux. "My wife and I are here on vacation."

"How very fortunate for you, sir. I'm here to read the newspaper if it's all the same to you."

"If what's all the same? The newspaper?" queried Betsy-May. "No, sir. Don't recognize that paper. Not the *Morgantown Sentinel* that's for sure. Looks to be in English, though. That English-English or American-English you readin'?"

Pinky shot me a glance like he thought maybe I'd provide some buffer to the assault. Fat chance of that.

Willard reached his hand out clear across Betsy-May and myself. "I'm Willard C. Calhoun, retired United States Navy," he offered. "Pleased to make your acquaintance. You ever in one of them Jap-o-nese prison camps? I was. Could be we've met before. Sorry, I didn't get your name, buddy. Willard C. Calhoun here."

"Excuse me," I said, looking at Pinky and then towards Willard. "Why don't we just exchange seats here, and you folks can be together."

"Oh, that's very kind of you, sir," said Betsy-May

"Mighty kind, indeed," said Willard. "We'll just scoot down one and you can have my stool. Got it nice and warm for ya, pal."

"Oh now, please," said Pinky, obviously flustered.

As the exchange of positions was taking place, I overheard Betsy-May whisper to Willard, "Maybe he doesn't want to talk to us, dear."

"Oh sure he do, sugar-plum. 'Member what I told you 'bout these English fellers. Just got to prime the pump a bit. You wait and see."

Personally, I could hardly wait.

Reluctantly, Pinky shook hands with Willard and said his name was "Ian."

"Ian, it's a downright pleasure to make your acquaintance. This here's my wife Betsy-May. We're from West Virginia. Over here on the vacation of a lifetime. 'Bout as far from West Virginia as a person can get without leaving the planet I reckon. What brings you to this neck of the woods?"

"I came here to read the newspaper."

"You from England, ain't ya?"

"That would be correct, sir."

"I knew it! I could tell from the sound of your voice that you was an Englishman," said Betsy-May. "Never met me a real live Englishman before. Seen 'em in the movies a' course, but it sure is excitin' to actually be sittin' next to one. Suppose you probably met a million folks from America before, uh Ian?"

"Not quite a million, ma'am."

"Ha! 'Not quite a million.' You hear that, sugar-plum? That's that English humor fer ya. Dry. Dry as powder. I love it. Sees, like I was saying before, I spent some time as guest of the Jap-o-nese in one a them POW camps during WW Two. Mean little bastards, them Japs, I don't mind sayin'. Quite a few of you English fellers there as well. Some a them were pretty funny. Kept me laughin' at times when I didn't much feel like it."

"Is that a fact?."

"Oh, you betcha, Ian. Another fact 'bout them English fellers is that they were polite. Always polite and respectful no matter how difficult the conditions were. I admired them for that, know what I mean, Ian?"

"Well, it hasn't always been my impression, but it's kind of you to say so, Willard."

"Don't mind saying so at all, Ian. It's the truth. At least in my experience, anyways. Thus far, that is. Mind if Betsy-May and I buy you a drink?"

"Ah . . . no. No, I don't mind at all. Blasted newspaper!"

"Ain't read a newspaper in years, Ian, made me feel better 'bout myself or the world around me. What'll it be, buddy?"

"Gin and tonic, if you please."

"Our pleasure. Think I'll have a Scotch myself. How 'bout you, sugar. "Another one of them tropical concoctions?"

"No. One of these was enough, dear. Like to have a gin and tonic. Good enough for Ian, it's good enough for me. When in Bangkok, do as the English do. Ha! Seems to me I heard that before."

"George Orwell, Betsy-May," said Ian. "It's from a book called *Burmese Days*. 'When in Burma, do as the British do,' he wrote."

"Could do worse. Yes sir, Ian, people could do worse than doin' as the British do. 'Specially in Burma these days from what I hear."

This was not developing into the scenario I had imagined. A cross-cultural divide was in the midst of being forged, and I felt moderately ashamed of myself for hoping otherwise. What kind of a man would prefer conflict in lieu of harmony? The kind of man, I supposed, who ends up spending his fiftieth birthday drinking alone, perhaps.

I decided to relocate from the bar to a table.

It was only 9:30 and I was still hoping that one or two of the people who knew of my Bamboo Bar birthday bash might join in the festivities. Of course, there weren't any festivities directly associated with my birthday, but I just throw that in for the hell of it.

The music was due to begin at 10:00 and the place was getting crowded. The only people still alone other than myself were the guy at the end of the bar in front of the band stage drinking cola-polluted whiskeys, and the old lady in the wheelchair. I noticed an available table in the upstairs lounge to the right—three short steps up. Thailand is littered with short steps that lead from one room or chamber to another. To my understanding, this is a consequence of the Thai's belief that these steps keep out evil spirits. I've been living here eight years and I continue to trip over the damn things several times a day, which might suggest that they aren't foolproof. It's a wonder I haven't broken my neck yet. Odds are that anyone who has as much trouble negotiating these demonic nuisances as I do is looked upon rather suspiciously by the natives. Fortunately, I advised the bartender of my intention to shift locations and he very graciously offered to have my libation delivered on a tray by one of the charming waitresses.

I tripped up the steps and sat down at the table. It was a low-rise rectangular affair with four wooden legs and a marble surface trimmed in wood—the same kind of wood the legs were made of, in case knowing that sort of thing is important to you. On the top of the table was a small green vase of orchids and a gold-plated ashtray in a shape that reminded me of the little hat worn by an organ-grinder's monkey. The small green vase, by the way, was made of celadon, which is a fine, glazed porcelain distinguished by its cracked eggshell exterior, and is handcrafted by artisans from Northwest Thailand. My knowledge of this subject, the sum total of which is on display in the preceding sentence, was acquired while I was visiting friends in the northern capital of Chiang Mai a dozen years ago.

The friends to which I refer are a married couple of mixed racial heritage. He being English and she, Thai. They live on one of the most beautiful estates in the region. There are four Thai-style homes of varying dimensions resting aloft teakwood pillars, set amidst a garden of tall, thick bamboo shoots, sweet smelling jasmine and frangipani, towering shade trees, sandstone walking paths, a grassy knoll that drapes down to the banks of the River Ping, and an assortment of other traditional whatnots like large colorful water basins and coconut-shell ladles that help to establish an atmosphere of enchanting serenity.

One of the many pleasurable aspects of visiting this delightful couple is that I get a separate house of my own in which to reside. I like that arrangement. In fact, I'd be happy to visit more people if they were willing and able to provide similar accommodations. It's much easier to make yourself at home, as the saying goes, when you actually have your own home and are, thus, not constantly exposed to the domestic idiosyncrasies of your hosts.

A sadder fact to consider, however, is that one of the main reasons I am not often invited to visit people is probably because they don't have a separate and distant vault in which to store me.

On this particular visit, after making myself very much at home for three days, my hosts decided it might be a good idea if I vacated the premises for a few hours. To expedite the matter, they arranged to have a *tuk-tuk* escort me to the local craft colony outside of town.

A *tuk-tuk* is a three wheeled, open sided, motorized vehicle that makes a great deal of noise, spews copious quantities of toxic pollutants into the air, and is invariably under the control of a helmsman whose behavior demonstrates an extremely low regard for the sanctity of human life, including his own. It took over an hour to reach our destination, by which time my eardrums were so rattled I could scarcely hear myself coughing to death.

Anyway, that is when, where, and how I learned all I know about celadon porcelain, and the recollection inspired me to drain what was left of my second Irish whiskey and order a third one. I managed to do that while simultaneously flicking a bit of cigarette ash into the gold-plated ashtray. Regretably, I have nothing to say on the subject of gold other than that I do not possess any and wish to God that I did. A statement revealing both a deficiency in my financial net worth, as well as my character I suppose.

There were two sloping armchairs beside the table where I'd settled. Like the other chairs in this three-step-up lounge, they are upholstered in an imitation leopard-skin fabric. The cushioned seat was approximately six inches thick and exceedingly agreeable to sit on. The vantage point it offered was equally agreeable. I had a view of the bar, the main room, and the band stage, all being three steps down from where I perched.

The three members of the band began assembling shortly before ten o'clock and were tuning their instruments as my third Irish whiskey arrived. The only reason I knew it was shortly before ten o'clock is because I noticed the wristwatch of the waitress as she delivered the fresh libation, removed the dead one, and cleaned the gold-plated ashtray. I haven't worn a wristwatch in years. For the most part, they're a source of annoyance as far as I'm concerned. A common lament of those who are inclined by nature to industry is that the 24 hours in a day are not enough for them to accomplish all their tasks. Nature was clearly not so generous in her bestowal of an inclination towards industry when she fashioned my character. On the contrary, *my* common lament is that there are just too damn many hours in a day to cope with. I'm usually asleep eight to ten hours a day, so that's not a problem. Then I'll spend an hour lying in bed after I wake up in the morning and another hour lying in bed before I fall asleep at night. Sleeping is a big part of my life.

Sleeping is also healthy for you. A person who gets plenty of sleep lives longer. I read that in a newspaper once, so I rest my case. Half my life revolves around sleeping, and that's fine by me. The challenge is what to do with the rest of the hours in the day. I only eat two meals; read for a couple hours; walk to the store for food; swim in the pool early each morning and, again, later in the afternoon; maybe watch a movie on television if there's a good one on, which there usually isn't; and that, in a nutshell, comprises the basic activities of my day. Unfortunately, however, a 24-hour period of time allows for a great deal more activity than can be comprised in a nutshell. There are just too damn many hours in a day for me to do what I do, and that doesn't seem fair. Why should my life be debited 24 hours every day when I only use 17 or 18 of them? If there were any justice in the matter, I'd only be forty years old now instead of fifty. I've been overcharged by ten years.

A sympathetic acquaintance of mine—and believe you me, I don't have many—suggested that I acquire a hobby. There were, of course, a couple of destitute families in Cambodia that I supported for a while. That was sort of a hobby. As it turned out, after two and a half years, all I had really accomplished was creating additional idle time for the adults of these two families to indulge their own hobbies of gambling and drunkenness. The unfortunate children were compelled to drop out of school and ended up back on the streets begging, just as they had been when I first met them.

Following that debacle I decided to consider a less stressful hobby, so I took up crossword puzzles. I've learned a lot from doing crossword puzzles. For instance, I've learned that Thomas Edison's middle name was Alva and that a fencing sword is called an 'epee.' Granted, the acquisition of that kind of knowledge is not going to put one in the position of changing the world, but then, I'm not especially interested in changing the world. I've enough trouble remembering to change my underwear every day. Yesterday I nearly broke my wrist holding up a corner of the mattress while changing the bed sheets. Changing the world is just out of the question.

The *Bangkok Post* and the *International Herald Tribune* are the two publications I resort to for this current hobby of mine. Six crossword puzzles a week is my limit. The *Herald Tribune* puzzles become progressively more difficult as the week goes on. Wednesday is as far as I get with those. The puzzles in the *Bangkok Post* are simply too easy to bother with Monday through Friday, so I concentrate on the Saturday one and the two on Sunday. That's my regimen; Monday, Tuesday, and Wednesday—the *Herald Tribune* puzzles. Saturday and Sunday—the *Bangkok Post*. I do, however, hold the other puzzles of the week on reserve for psychological purposes. When I start getting too fat-headed about myself, I'll make an attempt at the *Herald Tribune's* puzzles of Thursday, Friday, or Saturday. I fail miserably, of course, and my humility is restored. If, on the other hand, I find myself in exorbitant despair with regard to my level of intelligence, the Monday through Friday puzzles in the *Bangkok Post* provide a welcome tonic. These are merely a couple of tricks I've developed to maintain a healthy equilibrium, and I pass them on, free of charge, for what they're worth.

Doing crossword puzzles has been a good hobby for me. Oh, and before I forget, today I learned what an arachnid is. It's a spider! 'Arachnid' was the clue for 12-across requiring six letters. I don't even know how to pronounce the word. Never seen it before. But, I figured out that the second, fourth, and sixth letters were 'p', 'd,' and 'r' respectively, so what else could an arachnid be, other than a spider, right? How about that! Lucky for me the clue wasn't 'spider' and the answer 'arachnid.'

Two of the three people at a table next to mine got up to leave. They hugged and kissed and all that rigmorole. An elderly gentleman remained and re-seated himself facing in my direction. He was dressed very smartly in an open necked, long sleeve, black silk shirt with Kelly green pinstripes, light gray flannel trousers, black tasseled loafers, and a cotton, sapphire-colored necktie cordoned through the belt loops and knotted loosely just to the left of center—*a la* Fred Astaire. A moment passed before our glances crossed paths and we nodded cordially at each other. He asked me if I was enjoying myself this evening and I said so far so good and how's by you? He replied that he'd been enjoying himself quite nicely up till then. Said the female adjunct of the partnership that had just departed was celebrating her birthday and I said well, what do you know, so am I. "Half-century mark today," I added.

"Fifty years old, uh? Well, first of all, happy birthday to you."

"Thanks. You're the only person all day that's wished me a happy birthday."

"How many other people have you told?"

"None."

"I see. Was your picture in the newspaper or on television or something? I mean, what do you want?"

"Right."

"I envy you being fifty. It's a great age to be. I'll be 77 next month, and as I look back I can honestly say that my fifties were the best ten years of my life."

"Really."

"Oh, absolutely. People don't expect much from a man after he turns fifty, and as far as I'm concerned, having to cope with other people's expectations is a royal pain in the ass. They're distracting. And by that I mean other people's expectations too often distract a man from what his true purpose in life was meant to be. You have your parents' expectations, then your teachers and your peers, then you get married and have to deal with your wife's expectations. Maybe you have children, and before you know it they've begun to foster expectations of you. It can go on forever until one day you wake up to find out that most of those people with all their expectations of you are gone. Either they're dead or they simply don't care anymore. Is this making any sense to you, young man?"

"A little bit, and you're the second person tonight to call me a young man. I like that."

"Youth, of course, is a relative term to a certain degree. By the time you're my age, most people will be younger than you are."

"With the way medical science is progressing, by the time I get to be your age, pal, I might still feel fairly youthful."

"Well, I'll drink to that. What you got there?"

"Jameson on the rocks."

"Irish whiskey, uh? You Irish?"

"Ancestors were. It's in the blood. That and a touch of Welsh."

"Nice combination. I'm Jewish, myself. Jewish through and through. Have you ever heard it said that the Irish are the 'Lost Tribe of Israel'?"

"Yeah, I've heard that before."

"And?"

"Well, aside from being Irish, I was also raised Catholic, and that's enough of a guilt trip without worrying about being Jewish on top of it."

"Yes, I see your point. Think I'll join you for a Jameson, myself. Little bit of Irish won't do my blood any harm."

"Now tell me more about why your fifties were the happiest years of your life," I said. "No more of other people's expectations to live up to, was that it?"

"Basically."

"How about your own expectations?"

"No such thing, my friend. A man doesn't come into this world with any expectations for himself. They are products of the society in which he is raised. Parents, teachers, peers, mates, children, etcetera—like I said before. When you reach fifty, most of those people, one way or another, are gone. That's when you come face to face with a world which doesn't much give a damn anymore what you do. At fifty, you've either fulfilled their expectations or you haven't, and whatever you do beyond that is sort of a bonus. It's unexpected. To be in a position to do the unexpected was a thrilling prospect for me, and a fifty-year-old man is capable of doing many things that the world doesn't expect. You're entering a period of your life that will be full of surprises and enormous gratification."

"So, you've lived to see a lot of changes in this world, haven't you?"

"Oh, I certainly have."

"Automobiles, jet-airplanes, rocket ships to the moon, TV and movies, computers, medical advances against disease, nuclear power and, of course, the rising hemlines and plunging cleavage of female fashions."

"And a few wars, of course," he added.

"Ah, yes. Man's inhumanity. . . ."

"Don't be silly. War is very much a part of Man's humanity. In fact, there is nothing that Man does, whether we like it or not, that isn't part of his humanity. How could it possibly be otherwise?"

"That's a rather cynical assessment, don't you think?"

"I prefer to think of it as a logical assessment. Human behavior is human behavior. Just because someone may not approve of it doesn't make it inhuman. It simply isn't in Man's nature to do anything inhuman."

"So war and cruelty and crime and corruption are here to stay, as you see it."

"I'm afraid so. As are episodes of peace and kindness and fair play. All part of the human condition, birthday boy. In my life, I've pretty much seen it all. What a grand spectacle!"

"I assume you've been more than just a spectator."

"Oh sure. Not much choice. We're all players. I was married for twenty some years; no children. Made quite a bit of money in the commercial real-estate business. Wife left me for a younger man and she was ten years younger than I was at the time."

"At the time? Is she no longer ten years younger than you?"

"Not exactly. She's dead now, but I appreciate your logic."

"I was hoping you would."

"She was 41 when she left me, and dead of Alzheimer's disease a few years ago."

"Alzheimer's disease, uh?"

"Yeah. You know how to spell that?"

"No idea."

"Did you ever?"

"Nope, sorry."

"Don't be sorry," he said. "The thing that bothers me is, I used to know how to spell it and now I don't."

"Ah. Not a good sign, old-timer. Better drink up and be merry while you've still got a few wits about you. Ready for another shot of the Irish?"

"No thanks. Eleven o'clock is my bedtime, and I've a few matters to tend to before then. Been nice talking with you, though. You have a happy birthday and enjoy your fifties."

I flagged the waitress for another Jameson and settled in with my own company again. I don't usually have any major objections to my own company but still, it would have been fine by me if the old man had stayed around for one more drink. I was even on the verge of offering to buy it for him. If I'd known ahead of time that he was adamant about leaving, I *would* have offered to buy him a drink. It's not often one gets an opportunity for a display of generosity that doesn't end up costing money. Must be something to that rumor about the Irish being the lost tribe of Israel.

Seems to me I prefer the company and conversation of people older than myself. One thing I know is that I miss my father. Can't think of anyone I'd rather have been with drinking Irish whiskey at the Bamboo Bar on my fiftieth birthday than him. It's a strange feeling for me to realize that he was dead at the age of 56 and so, if I were able to conjure his presence this evening, his company and conversation would be that of a contemporary. Of course, having been on the other side of the curtain for the past 22 years, I suppose he might be in a position to add a more enlightened perspective.

Midway through my fourth Irish whiskey with Gershwin's "I've Got Rhythm" just having finished jazzing the ambience, it was announced that the play reading was about to begin. The play was scheduled to be read in three installments by a small ensemble of American actors. It was titled *The Rock Bottom Good-bye* and written by the aforementioned Genevieve Langdon.

The lights were slightly dimmed as two women and a man sat down on barstools that had been placed upon the band stage. A voice from offstage said, "Good evening ladies and gentlemen and welcome to the Bamboo Bar. Please allow me to make the following brief statement before our play reading begins:

"Cellphone conversations between loved-ones in crisis should be rehearsed. A man on the top floor of a burning building calls his wife. Death is imminent. He has only moments to decide whether to jump out a window or burn alive. In either case, he's going to be dead very soon. So, he calls his wife to say good-bye. . . ."

With the sound of a phone ringing, the reading commenced. . . .

"Good afternoon, Mansfield residence."
"Maria, this is Mr. Mansfield. Is my wife there, please?"
"Oh, hello Mr. Mansfield. How are you?"
"Maria, I'm kind of in a hurry. Is my wife there?"
"She's upstairs with little Billy. He just wake from his nappy. You like I have her call you back?"
"Maria, put my wife on the phone. NOW!"

"Yes, Mr. Mansfield. No need to yell."

"Sorry, Maria."

"That's all right. Are you okay?"

"Maria, PLEASE, my wife!"

(Pause)

"Hello, William. Listen, can I call you back . . ."

"Muffy?"

"Yes, William, it's me. I'm just a little busy . . ."

"Muffy, I (cough) love you!"

"Oh, aren't you sweet."

"I love (cough, cough) you so much!"

"William, I do wish you'd quit smoking. Just listen to that cough of yours."

"I can't help it, darling."

"Well, if you really loved me, I think you *could* help it. And, think of the children . . ."

"Muffy, damn it, I *am* thinking of the (cough) children. I love (cough, cough) all our darlings."

"So quit smoking then, William. Oh, and please don't forget about Sarah's tennis lesson this evening. You promised to stop by in time to watch . . ."

"Muffy, darling, I'm afraid (cough) that won't be possible. You see . . ."

"Won't be possible! Now, damn it William, you promised to watch her for a while and bring her home."

"I can't."

"You mean you're going to be working late again tonight? This is getting just a little ridiculous. Every night last week . . . please William, would you stop that damn coughing into my ear!"

"Oh, Muffy darling,, (cough, cough) I love you (hacking) so much!"

"Yes dear, I know you do. . . . Maria . . . Maria, I hear little Billy crying . . . please go see what his trouble is. William, Billy's teething is getting worse . . ."

"I love little (choking) Billy . . ."

"My, aren't we full of love this morning, William. Could you stop by a drugstore on your way home and pick up some more of that gum-numbing medicine ?"

"(choking and coughing) I, I . . ."

"Jesus, William, put out the damn cigarette!"

"It's not the cigarette, damn it!"

"Well, what the hell . . . are you smoking cigars again?"

"It's the building, Muffy."

"You're smoking the fucking building. . . ? Jesus Christ, William!"

"It's on fire, you insensitive bitch!"

"Insensitive bitch! Well, thank you very much, you dickwad!"

"The building is full of (choking) smoke. It's on fire!"

"Fire?"

"Yes."

"Your building is on fire?"

"Yes, darling."

"Oh no, William."

"Yes. And would you please stop calling me William?"

"You prefer dickwad?"

"Bitch!"

"Asshole! How do like that. . . ? You like 'asshole' better than William?"

"Darling, please. I'm sorry. I just wish (cough, hack) . . . I just wish you'd call me sweetheart or honey or something like that. I love you, Muffy—really I do. I want to hold you so much!"

"Will . . . sweetheart, is your building really on fire? Oops, there's somebody on the other line. Just a . . ."

"Darling no—don't put me on hold!"

"Just a second, William . . ."

(More coughing and hacking and choking.)

"Oh my God, William . . . sweetheart, my dearest . . . that was Sheryl Phillips . . . you know, Brad's wife. Well, listen to me—of course you know who Sheryl is, don't you, William. Couldn't keep your paws off her at the Charity Ball last month. Anyway, never mind about that . . . she saw on the news . . . your building. . . . Oh sweetheart, your building *is* on fire!"

"Yes, darling."

"And you're on the top floor! Can you get out?"

"It's too late. The fire's coming up. All the exits are in flames."

"Oh no, no, no!"

"Did Sheryl sound upset?"

"Fuck Sheryl, you dickwad . . . sweetheart!!"

"I never fucked Sheryl, darling. Never!"

"Swear?"

"Honestly, darling. I swear I never fucked her."

"Oh, now I feel just horrible. I was sure you and Sheryl were . . ."

"No, my love. It was just an innocent flirtation. You know, like you and Brad had going."

"Oh, William . . ."

"That *was* just an innocent flirtation between you and Brad, right?"

"Pretty much so, sweetheart."

"Pretty (choking) much so!"

"Well, that's how it started out."

"That's how we started out, you wanton hussy!"

"Please, sweetheart . . ."

"Don't call me sweetheart!"

"Maria . . . Maria where are you? Damn that woman!"

"Yes, Mrs. Mansfield?"

"Don't you hear little Billy crying? Please get a Popsicle out of the freezer and have him suck on it."

"Muffy, I can't see anymore. The smoke is everywhere."

"Oh my sweet, sweet William. Can you climb out the window?"

"And do what? Damn it!"

"Well, hang there for a while. Maybe a helicopter . . ."

"Darling, I'm on the eighty-eighth floor. (Choking.) It's either jump or burn to death. What do you suggest?"

"Well, either way I guess we can forget about an open casket. . . . Oh dear, I'm sorry. That was just a little joke."

"Ha, ha, ha . . ."

"Maybe jump . . . yes. I can't bear the thought of you burning alive. Besides, you always wanted to fly—isn't that right my love?"

"Not out a window for Christsakes!"

"Mrs. Mansfield, the grocery boy is here. Shall I have him come in through the back door?"

"Yes, Maria. Please. You take care of it. Mr. Mansfield is burning up."

"Oh, my husband gets that way sometimes, too. Don't you worry about him. He'll be just fine."

"Thank you, Maria. Sweetheart, are you still there?"

"Still here, darling. I've decided to jump. The flames are in my office now. Oh, it's so damn hot!"

"Take the cellphone with you, dearest. Then we can talk while you're on the way down."

"Count with me, darling. One, two, three and I jump."

"Okay, dear."

"Ready. . . . One . . . two . . . three . . . wooooo!"

"Honest . . . you never fucked Sheryl?"

"Nooooooooooo!"

"I love you, sweetheart!"

"I love you, tooooo!"

"Brad was just a great lay. That's all, sweetheart. I never loved him. It's you . . ."

"Whoooorrrre!"

(Line goes dead.)

"Whore? How dare you call me a . . . William, are you there. . . ? Damn you, speak to me. . . ! Maria . . . Maria! Catch that grocery boy and ask him to pick up a tube of gum-numbing medicine for little Billy."

"I thought Mr. Mansfield was going to do that on his way home."

"Mr. Mansfield won't be home tonight, Maria."

And that was the end of Act I. Several people around the bar seemed to get a kick out of it, but it was my impression that most weren't paying much attention. Nevertheless, I thought it was an amusing bit of entertainment and I was looking forward to the next installment. In the meantime, I remained sitting by myself and ordered another drink.

I enjoy drinking alone.

A common speculation is that a person who enjoys drinking alone is either an alcoholic or well on his way to becoming one. I don't consider myself an alcoholic, but then I've never met a practicing alcoholic who did consider himself to be one. Maybe I am and maybe I'm not. There are certainly worse things a guy could be. Heroin addicts and serial killers are far more frightful characters than I am. I don't even know why I bother to mention this. I live alone, I eat alone, I go to movies alone—most of my life I've been alone. So, it isn't exactly extraordinary that I should find myself alone on my fiftieth birthday. What I have found, however, is that nothing much happens to people who spend most of their lives alone. We tend to be fairly cognizant observers of what happens around us but, still, nothing much happens to us. We're unengaged you might say.

When I was half as old as I am tonight, I used to hang out at a saloon on North Avenue in Chicago. It was called O'Rourke's. I like saloons. The Bamboo Bar is not a saloon. It's a bar. It's a good bar, but it's not a saloon; not by my definition, anyway.

A saloon is a drinking-hole—it's an oasis of booze. Saloons don't serve food. They don't even serve peanuts or pretzels. Not a real saloon. They don't provide entertainment other than maybe a jukebox and a pinball machine.

That's what they had at O'Rourke's—a jukebox and a pinball machine. Most of the joint was made out of wood. The floor was wood, the ceiling was wood, the walls were wood, the bar and barstools were wood, the booths were wood. . . . Yeah, like I said, most of the joint was made out of wood.

It wasn't an expensive operation. O'Rourke's didn't waste a lot of money on lights, and there wasn't any air-conditioning. There were ceiling fans, though. Wooden propellers, of course.

One concession they did make to comfort was radiators. The place was well heated in the winter, and in Chicago that's important.

The bartender's name was Kevin; Kevin Kearney. He never had much to say—not to me, anyway. He was in his mid-fifties back then, so he's probably dead by now. Might just as well have been dead then, as far as his talent for conversation was concerned. Not your typical Irishman in that regard. But he sure knew how to pour a drink, I'll say that much for him. And that's another part of my definition about a saloon. It *pours* drinks. You don't go to a saloon for cocktails or the sort of fruity Polynesian contrivances that are served here in the Bamboo Bar. The only mixers that O'Rourke's provided were water and soda. I mean, in a real saloon like O'Rourke's, a Scotch on the rocks is considered a mixed drink.

Guinness was a mainstay of the joint. With a name like O'Rourke's, it should have been and it was. Draft Guinness, that is; not Guinness in a can. Canned Guinness is what you can find at a few of the Irish bars in Bangkok. Of course, they're not really Irish bars, but they have Irish names. They cater to tourists on a tourist budget who for some reason like the idea of going to a bar with an Irish name and drinking a couple of exorbitantly priced aluminum cans of Guinness while they're on holiday in Thailand. It doesn't make much sense to me and I don't suppose these people are especially concerned that it should. Guy sitting by himself, drinking alone on his fiftieth birthday—who cares what the hell he thinks.

The Guinness at O'Rourke's came in steel kegs hooked up by a black rubber hose to the bar tap. Now, it's my understanding that the proper word to describe the procedure of transferring draft beer from a keg to a glass is 'draw.' One does not 'pour' a draft beer; one 'draws' a draft beer. Sounds kind of artistic, doesn't it? And, in fact, there is an art to it. A guy just doesn't fall out of a tree knowing how to draw a good pint of Guinness. It requires skill and patience. Kevin was a master at it. He knew just what angle to tilt the glass against the tap, how much to draw and let it settle before drawing more, and how to serve it with a perfect-looking creamy head of caramel colored froth. This process itself could take as long as three or four minutes to get it right. Depending on your mood, that could be enough time to finish off a shot of whiskey while you waited. A good saloon will put you in that kind of mood.

Suddenly I heard groaning and panting noises come from a table off to my right. I turned as nonchalantly as I could. Naturally, this took some time. The first thing I noticed was an open bottle of champagne in a silver ice bucket. Resting up against the ice bucket was a gold-trimmed card which read: *"Congratulations on your wedding and enjoy your honeymoon. All the best from the management of the Oriental Hotel."*

I was rather pleased with myself for being able to read that message given the fact that it was at least twenty feet away. Obviously the ol' peepers are still in pretty good condition. What I noticed next, however, made me reconsider that assessment. The couple at the table appeared to be making love. Could that possibly be? I blinked a few times and re-focused. Sure enough, my eyes had not deceived me. They *were* making love.

The couple appeared to be in their early thirties and definitely from out of town. Judging from the passionate tone of expressions, my guess was that they were Dutch. I had a Dutch girlfriend once who sounded very much the same. We had met on Koh Samui, fallen deeply in love, and remained so for what, at the time, seemed like an eternity. According to the number of blank entries in my diary, however, it only lasted for ten days. I don't bother with the damn diary when I'm in love. She dumped me for an Italian stud and the two of them left Samui for a mating tour in the jungles of Borneo. Got eaten alive for all I know. Anyway, the sounds from the woman at the table to my right reminded me of this bittersweet chapter of my usually unattended existence. "Extraordinary how potent cheap music is . . ." as Noel Coward would have it.

The woman, wearing a conservative, mid-calf-length yellow chiffon skirt, was sitting in a side-saddle fashion on her husband's lap. The skirt itself served as a sort of canopy shielding the carnal high jinks that they both were clearly enjoying. I was rather enjoying it myself, although trying to be discreet. Discretion is one of several virtues I've come to appreciate while living in Thailand the past nine years. Tolerance is another one. The man winked at me as he caught my eye. Nice touch, I thought, as I returned to my Irish whiskey.

A truism if ever there was such a thing is the one which postulates that, generally speaking, acts of sexual congress by one method or another are characteristic of all relationships between male and female members of the various animal kingdom species. As Cole Porter lyricized, "Birds do it, bees do it, even educated fleas do it." Up until very recently, this activity was the sole means by which the species managed to propagate themselves. The ministers of modern science, however, have now made it possible for creatures to proliferate without having to copulate. For nearly 2,000 years, one of the most distinguishing features of the greatest holy man this side of Buddha was his alleged 'virgin birth.' These days there are a thriving number of sheep and cows prancing upon the premises who can make the same claim. Furthermore, if the sexual predisposition of Mr. Porter and his mates were to become the norm, then all our mothers would be virgins. Assuming, of course, that we would have the foggiest idea who our mothers were.

Such a set of circumstances is not likely to happen within the realm of any species other than the human one. And there is a very simple explanation for that. Namely, it is my suspicion that human beings are the only species who are the least bit concerned with the physical aspects of their prospective mates when it comes to engaging in the sexual congress hitherto necessary for one generation to follow another. I do not believe that birds and bees and fleas, regardless of the extent of their education, are at all compelled to 'do it' with one prospective mate over another as a consequence of mutual physical attraction. In fact, it might well be argued that the majority of animal kingdom creatures are pretty damn ugly. Beach dogs and stray bitches are a classic example.

Humans, on the other hand, are obsessed by the physical allure of, not only others, but themselves as well. Men become aroused by the shape and size of a woman's breasts. Women ogle men's buttocks and fantasize about large penises. Both sexes often go to great lengths to enhance these respective physical attributes for the sole purpose of making themselves more attractive. They even concern themselves about what their offspring will look like based upon the appearance of possible mates. I've never had the impression that your typical farm animals give a shit what their litter look like—which may be one good reason why the offspring of these creatures are referred to as litter.

It may be of interest to point out that these ruminations were inspired during an evening not long ago while I was sucking on bottles of beer at a Nana Plaza go-go bar called Lollipop. I found myself wondering about the obvious lack of similar venues available to our fellow beasts within the animal kingdom. There are no camel, dog, rat, or rhino go-go bars as far as I know. Male hippopotamuses do not hang out at hippo go-go bush bars quaffing bottles of fermented swamp water ogling the mammary glands and hindquarters of unclad hippo girls uncapping bottles of soda pop with their vaginas. And it's unlikely that one peacock has ever said to another peacock, "Hey, check out the tits on that hen!"

Rodents don't have breast implants, or sows tummy tucks, or hyenas face-lifts and nose jobs. There simply isn't a lot of demand for cosmetic surgery among animals other than humans.

So, what's my point?

Frankly, I'm not sure yet. Perhaps one will occur to me later. Sometimes I find myself just ruminating upon quirky observations for no particular reason at all. If nothing else, it helps pass the time in an entertaining fashion . . . entertaining to me, anyway.

Okay, I admit it. I talk to myself. Not, as a rule, out loud, but nevertheless. . . . It's a terrible shame, as far as I'm concerned, that the art of conversation is so rarely practiced anywhere, anymore. If I didn't have myself to talk with, I'd soon lose the ability to verbally communicate altogether. Fortunately, one of the greatest blessings bestowed upon me is that I enjoy my own company. Unfortunately, the vast majority of people don't enjoy their own company, and I suspect that many of the problems of this world are a consequence of the fact that these people have nobody else to converse with. Too many people have lost the knack for conversation due to lack of practice. Once again, we have become an image-oriented society. We are spectators . . . we watch. Television, movies, and photography—these are the bogus 'art forms' that we indulge and so pathetically rely upon to define our world and our own sense of self-worth within that world.

Speaking of Cole Porter, the singer finished her first set with an up-tempo version of his "I've Got You Under My Skin." It turned out to be an appropriate segue for what happened next. No sooner had the band members retired from the bar to smoke a bit of weed on the terrace along the river when a gunshot rang out. Sounded like a .38 caliber to me, although I'm certainly not an expert on such matters. Clearly, however, a Thai gentleman dressed in a brown cotton sport coat and beige trousers had somehow managed to get under the skin of another Thai gentleman wearing a navy-blue silk blazer and green trousers. Upon appraising the situation, I was immediately reminded of Frank Sinatra's dictum that it was most unfashionable for a man to wear brown after six o'clock in the evening, and I believe Sinatra was respected for his sartorial elegance nearly as much as he was for his various other talents. That's not to suggest that a man who chooses to attire himself in brown clothes after six o'clock in the evening ought to be shot, but having said that, I don't think a venue as stylish as the Bamboo Bar was any worse off—at least in terms of its decorous environs—when the body was removed.

Lest this incidence belie my earlier contention that tolerance is a contagious virtue here in the Land of Smiles, it must be pointed

At the Bamboo Bar

out that a tendency towards precipitous acts of violence is also part of the Thai character. Tolerance has its limits, for Christsakes— or, Buddha's sake, as the sake may be.

What one needs to be aware of is that the limits to tolerance in Thailand are not very well marked. There are often no early warning signs. A Thai will suffer offense with a smile on his face up to a point that is often influenced by the amount of alcohol in his bloodstream. He's not likely to engage the offending party in loud, angry rebuke. That's considered bad form. When the point of tolerance has been exceeded, the offended Thai, still smiling, may very well pull out a gun and open fire. Such was the case tonight.

Shortly following the incident, two members of the hotel security staff dressed in dark suits and white shirts escorted the gunman out of the bar. Presumably, he would be requested to fill out a few forms and give his version of what occurred. The other three people in his party remained in their seats and were served an additional round of beverages compliments of the house. Gracious hospitality is a trademark of five-star Bangkok hotels. The surviving members of the unfashionably clad gentleman's ensemble declined a similar offer of free drinks and accompanied the body off the premises. Apparently, he had been the life of the party and they figured it was time to call it a night. Tough to be the life of the party when you're. . . . Well, never mind. No cheap shots out of me, folks.

As the commotion settled down, I decided to go to the men's room and relieve the bladder. There isn't an *en suite* toilet at the Bamboo Bar. You have to walk outside, take a left through the hallway, and enter the lobby. Two more left turns place you into the men's room, and that would be true even if you weren't a man. It's very nice. Quite swank, actually. A couple of urinals; three toilet stalls; four wash basins in front of a large mirror; orchids floating in little china bowls; and a wicker basket of fresh, clean and pressed cotton towels—'towelettes,' I believe is the proper name for them, although that's not a word listed in my dictionary. They're hand towels. About 12-inches square, that sort of thing. Only to be found in the grandest of Bangkok's five-star-hotel lavatories, and not to be confused with the disposable though scented versions available to favored customers of some Bangkok go-go bars.

I sidled up to one of the urinals, and while fishing out the typical Irishman's 'angry inch,' I realized Willard C. Calhoun was going about his business right beside me.

"Howdy, pardner" he said. "Hell of a scene in the bar few minutes back, uh? These Thais are sort of a touchy bunch, ain't they?"

"Didn't see it happen," I said, "but I heard the gunshot. Any idea what it was about?"

"Well, me and the missus was sittin' at a nearby table with an English bloke we'd just met. Pretty much mindin' our own business, tellin' war stories and such, but fer as I can make out, the dead man was eyeballin' the other man's girl. You could tell just from the way he was talkin' that he'd had a bit too much to drink. The dead man, I mean. Guess he asked the girl to dance with him fer one thing. Then he had a glass of pink champagne sent over . . . not to the girl—to the man. That's when words were exchanged between the two men and next thing ya know—bang! Don't much care fer pink champagne myself. How 'bout you?"

I expressed agreement with Willard on that issue, and he zipped himself up saying, "Men don't drink pink champagne where I come from. It's a sissy drink, know what I mean? He was insulting the other man, fer as I can figure."

"Causing the guy to lose face as they say around here," I suggested.

"Yep, I've heard that phrase. 'Face' is like what we call pride, ain't it?"

"Pretty much along the same lines."

We were in front of the mirror by then, washing our hands.

At the Bamboo Bar

"I just love these little towels, don't you?" said Willard. "Might take one with me as a souvenir. Think that'd be all right, pardner?"

"I don't think they'd miss one, pal. It'll be our little secret."

"'Course, I reckon if everybody took one, the hotel would probably go with those cheap paper towels like the less fancy places, so forgit it."

"Good for you."

"Well, see ya back in the bar. Maybe have a drink together if you like, later. Name's Willard, by the way. Willard C. Calhoun. Yours?"

"People call me Mac. Nice to meet you, Willard."

"Okay, Mac. Be seein' ya."

I waited a moment after he left, stuck a towelette in my pocket, and strolled back to the Bamboo Bar. The band members had reassembled and were playing the theme song from Peter Sellers' movie *A Shot in the Dark*. Musicians with a macabre sense of humor. I liked it.

There is something unmistakably redemptive about humor— even of the macabre variety. In another bar in another country they may have responded to the shooting death of a patron by playing some maudlin dirge and then closed down for the rest of the evening. That would have put a stamp of tragedy on the scene and lowered the curtain. To hell with tragedy, I say. Let the show go on!

The singer returned to the band stage and picked up the mike. . . .

"I was born in the South Bronx," she said. "Played some rough clubs in Harlem and the South Side of Chicago. Seen a good deal of violence in my time. Oh, believe you me, darlins, I been in amongst it more than I care to recollect. Now, let's not have any more of it here tonight. We gonna have some fun!"

Having said her peace, the band struck up "Luck Be a Lady Tonight," and away she sang.

The waitress brought over a fresh Irish whiskey carried on a silver tray. This time she also provided me with a new coaster to rest the glass upon. I very much like the coasters at the Bamboo Bar, and always take a couple of them with me when I leave. They're quite distinctive looking. Made of cardboard about three-square inches. The border is tan with black furry looking leopard spots, and the inside consists of four intersecting bamboo shafts. Green bamboo leaves sprout inward from the corners, and on the pale yellow center *"The Bamboo Bar"* is written in red script. At the bottom in small, standard black type is written *"The Oriental, Bangkok."*

Actually, I don't always take a couple of these coasters every time I visit the Bamboo Bar. That was an exaggeration. If I've been to the Bamboo Bar ten times in my life, maybe I've walked out with half a dozen all told. That's not so bad. They're mementos and I put them to good use, which means, I guess, that they're not exactly mementos. Mementos are keepsakes, right. . . ? Keepsakes aren't supposed to have any practical use other than as adornments of some kind. It's not like I have these coasters framed or hung as a pendant around my neck for Christsakes. I use them for my coffee cup in the morning, and evening cocktails. One time I had a friend over to my apartment for a few drinks. That doesn't happen often, so I let him use the coaster for his bottle of beer.

"You been to the Bamboo Bar?" he asked.

I said I had without trying to sound too pretentious about it.

"Nice coaster" he said. "Mind if I have it?"

So I gave it to him and that was that. Haven't invited him back since.

As for the towelette from the men's room, I was planning to use that also. In fact, just to prove to myself that I wasn't a kleptomaniac, I pulled it out of my pocket and blew my nose into it. I'd return it to the men's room laundry basket later.

These are the kind of niggling little concerns that besiege the mind of a loner such as myself. Why should I feel so compelled to justify or, at least, rationalize every single one of my actions that might be construed as being the least bit wayward? Other people certainly don't. I mean, here I am in one of the classiest bars in the world on a Saturday night. Over my right shoulder is a honeymoon couple consummating their marriage, and right in front of me a guy in a navy-blue blazer pulls out a gun and shoots someone. These people don't worry themselves into a sweat about lavatory towelettes and bar coasters. They're robust, carefree individuals. Why can't I be more like them?

I think too much. That's my problem. Fifty years old, I should let myself go. Live a little, damn it!

I picked up the coaster and flung it into the air. Just for the hell of it. After making several loops, it came to a perfect landing on the bar right beside a bowl of peanuts next to the whiskey and cola guy. He turned and looked at me. Seemed as if he knew instinctively that I was the perpetrator. I always get caught. That's the way it was at Campion, as well. Friend of mine blew up a toilet one night in the sophomore dormitory. Never got caught. A 100-year-old study hall burnt to the ground on a cold Sunday morning in February. Nobody was caught. Every time I forgot to make my bed they caught me. Then they kicked me out for having a "bad attitude." No wonder I'm not a robust and carefree soul.

The whiskey and cola guy picked up the coaster and walked over to my table.

"You lose this, by any chance?" he asked drolly.

"Not exactly," I said, feeling refreshingly bold. "In fact, chance had nothing to do with it. I flung it."

"I see," he said. "Any particular reason?"

"None whatsoever. It was an act of sheer fancy."

"You don't say."

"I do say. And, I also say you're welcome to join me for a drink if you don't mind."

Just then, the fellow looked over my shoulder. "Excuse me" he said, "have you noticed that couple behind you?"

"The one having sex at the back table?"

"Yes, that couple."

"They're on their honeymoon."

"Apparently they're quite in the midst of it. Perhaps I *shall* join you for a drink. It's like a three-ring circus in this place tonight. Murder, sex, flying coasters, that play reading . . ."

"And you gotta like the music, as well."

"That's true. Here's your coaster back. Just let me go get my drink from the bar and I'll join you."

"Ah, don't strain yourself. The waitress will take care of it. Have a seat."

And so he did.

By the time his drink was brought over, I had mentioned that it was my fiftieth birthday, and he insisted on buying me a drink instead of me buying him one. That started me thinking I should celebrate my fiftieth birthday more often.

The fellow was a young pup, 38 years of age, who came to Bangkok six months ago to do some research on a screenplay he was hoping to sell in Hollywood.

"It's sort of a cross-cultural thriller involving Southeast Asian warlords and American drug traffickers," he told me.

How original, I thought to myself. No doubt there's a bit of romance between some self-righteous, terminally glib American private investigator and an Asian beauty, I assumed.

"There's also a romantic sub-plot involving a Los Angeles detective and a beautiful young Thai woman," he added.

"Gosh," I said, "don't give the whole thing away before you've finished. That's supposed to be bad luck for a writer, isn't it?"

"Yeah, I guess you're right" he said. "God knows if there's one thing I don't need any more of, it's bad luck."

"Things not going your way lately, uh?"

"Lately? Bad luck's been the story of my life. It's a wonder I haven't blown my brains out by now."

"I'm sorry to hear that," I said, hoping that I wasn't going to have to hear any more of it.

"You haven't heard anything yet," he said.

Oh well.

"I mean, right out of the gate," he continued, "I was an abortion to begin with. How do you like them apples? Not exactly an auspicious introduction to the world, would you say?"

"You're speaking metaphorically, right. . . ?" I've always been a great admirer of people who have a talent for speaking and writing metaphorically.

"No I'm not speaking metaphorically. When I say I was an abortion, I mean it quite literally."

"And yet, you appear to have survived the ordeal. That's amazing. You must have been what's referred to as 'a late term' abortion. That's a bit of good luck, wouldn't you say?"

"The records indicate that I was approximately seven and a half months old when I was discovered in a trash can at a rest stop along the New Jersey Turnpike."

"The New Jersey Turnpike isn't a particularly scenic stretch of road, as I recall."

"It gets better the further south you go. Down along the Atlantic Coast."

"Yes. You're right about that. I was thinking more about the north end, outside of New York City."

"That's where I was found."

"Ah, too bad. Still, it's nice that you were found."

"Figure I was stuck there for two days. Fortunately it was right after a holiday weekend so there were plenty of food scraps and a couple half-full cans of soda pop. In fact, they say it was a can of cola with a straw in it that saved my life."

"Wow."

"Right after Labor Day weekend. How's that for irony?"

"Well, at least it wasn't Mother's Day. Probably not a date circled on your calendar, uh?"

"Not hardly. I don't circle any holidays on my calendar. Unlike you, I can't even be sure when my actual birthday was."

"Do abortions have birthdays?"

"Good point. I suppose not."

"Sorry. That was just kind of a joke."

"Never mind. I can take a joke. No point in livin' if you can't take a joke, that's for sure."

"That's the spirit, pal. And, after all, if you started out as an abortion, how much worse could things get?"

"You really want to know?"

I lied and said yes, but it was becoming clear to me that this guy had spent much of his adult life sitting alone at the end of a bar, drinking whiskey colas, and leaving in his wake a countless number of bartenders who wished they'd taken up a different profession. During the next twenty minutes he actually did manage to persuade me that having survived an abortion was no guarantee the worst was over with. Five years in an orphanage, 12 years in seven different foster homes, 18 months in a juvenile delinquent prison, two years in the army, and six and a half years as a cross-country truck driver hauling everything from used automobiles to various kinds of livestock. Along the way, he'd been physically and sexually abused, kicked out of two reform schools, and infected with the plague virus from a blood transfusion following the collapse of some scaffolding at a construction site he was working on.

Fortunately, the insurance claims and legal settlements with the construction company and hospital guaranteed that he would never have to work again as long as he lived. He explained a few of the financial details. . . .

"So, after all that, you're a millionaire," I said.

"That's right. But the medication I'm on is horrible. I live with fatigue and vomiting every day of my life. Every morning I wake up to a nightmare. It doesn't make any difference how much sleep I get; I wake up tired."

"You live with fatigue, as you said."

"Yes, as I said."

"And vomiting?"

"Well, of course, vomiting. In fact, if it weren't for the vomiting I probably wouldn't get out of bed, at all."

"No point, I suppose."

"So, I wake up each morning . . ."

". . . To a nightmare."

"Exactly."

"You're fatigued."

"Totally fatigued."

"No energy."

"None whatsoever."

"And then what?"

"Then I know I'm going to vomit, so I rush to the toilet and . . . throw up, vomit. That's what gets me out of bed."

"Otherwise?"

"Otherwise, I'd stay in bed all day."

"You could keep a bucket beside your bed."

"Yes, but there'd be the smell."

"How about a barf bag with a tight seal on it?" I was just trying to help.

"No, no. They require too much accuracy and co-ordination. And, well, I mean, it's good that I get out of bed. What the fuck am I going to do sitting in bed all day? I'm not Marcel fucking Proust or somebody."

Interesting that he knew of Proust.

"So, let me get this straight," I said. "You begin each day of your life feeling as if you're waking up to a nightmare, and then you vomit.'

"Yes."

"Your first thought is a nightmare."

"Ah uh."

"And your first deed is to barf."

"That is correct."

"Well, at least from that point on your day can only get better, right?" I knew that was a dumb question.

"Not necessarily," he said. "Some days just go downhill from there."

"How could you go downhill from waking up to a nightmare and vomiting? There is no hill down from that point."

"I start writing. It's a terribly frustrating process. I know this sounds strange considering what I've told you about myself, but every word I write is like giving birth to a child. Do you understand that? It's painstaking for God's sakes! I write five to seven hundred words a day. Fish don't even give birth to that many offspring. No living creature does. Oh, and it's not like they all come pouring out one after the other, either. Every single, solitary fucking word goes through the birthing process one at a time. I said to a woman friend of mine once, 'How would you like to go through labor five to seven hundred times a day?' Ha!"

"What did she say?"

"She said she was on the pill."

"That's funny."

"Yeah, she's a funny gal."

"You got anybody interested in this screenplay? If you've been drawing on any of your own experiences, it ought to make for a rather unusual movie."

"Guy I know in LA is in the business. He told me these sort of thrillers are a dime a dozen, but he'd look at it when I'm finished. It's all in the treatment, he said, and I'm working the story different than other people do."

"A different angle, uh?"

"Yeah. In my version of the genre, all the good guys die and the bad guys prevail."

"Clever. How about the girl?"

"She gets raped by a Burmese warlord and dies in childbirth."

"And the baby?"

"Not sure about that yet. I might let the baby live. You never know, if the movie's a success, there could be a sequel."

"Ah, good thinking. As a matter of fact, perhaps you wouldn't mind if I made a suggestion."

"All right."

"Are you familiar with those stories that fall within a category that I refer to as 'The Triumph of the Human Spirit'?"

"I have a hunch what you're talking about, but give me an example."

"Well, take a girl who comes from a broken home. Her father's a drunken bum who abandons the family before she's even born. The mother is a bottom-dwelling prostitute with an addiction to heroin who's forever being physically abused by the clientele. Frequently, the girl and her older sister are sexually molested. It's understood that the mother makes a bit of money on the side as a consequence of that activity. The older sister is eventually married off to some grisly character who parcels out her services to the porno industry. . . .

"That leaves the heroine of our story pretty much on her own except for the companionship of a mangy little stray dog which she adores with the greatest affection. Then one day . . ."

"Oh, don't tell me. The dog gets run over by a garbage truck, right?"

"I was going to say a pick-up truck but I like your idea better. It seems more apropos."

"The girl grows up, gets a scholarship to Harvard, graduates magna cum laude, and writes a book about her childhood . . ."

"The book sells ten million copies and wins a Pulitzer Prize. All the critics rave about her poetical yet simple use of the language, her humility, sense of humor, courage . . ."

"Lack of self-pity?"

"Oh, for sure that. No self-pity for Christsakes."

"A triumph of the human spirit?"

"Exactly."

"Yeah, I've read a couple of those books. They make me puke, and I puke enough as it is. So, what's your suggestion?"

"Create a new genre."

"How do you mean?"

"Well, a sort of 'Failure of the Human Spirit' genre."

"You mean like instead of playing the cards that are dealt you and making the most of it, you just fold?"

"Yeah."

"A lay-down-and-die kind of story."

"That's the spirit."

"Cool. I like that idea. Must be a lot of people in this world who could identify with that. I wonder if those kind of people buy books."

"Sure they do, and there must be millions of them. You'd be their favorite author. Think of all the money you could make."

"And the fame."

"Yeah. That, too."

"So maybe I should let the baby live and my follow-up book will be a chronicle of her miserable existence as an orphan in some squalid refugee camp."

"And in this refugee camp she endures a daily ration of unspeakable horrors."

"Endures, but never prevails."

"Oh goodness, no."

"But she complains a lot."

"Constantly."

"And reeks of self-pity."

"Absolutely. Reeks like a broken toilet on a Greek freighter that's been two months at sea."

"The story of a life with no redeeming value."

"None whatsoever."

"A complete failure of the human spirit."

"Precisely."

"Beautiful. Well listen, it's been nice talking to you," he said. "I'm going back to the bar. Enjoy the rest of your birthday."

"Thanks. And thanks for the drink. Sorry about the coaster."

"Hey, never a dull moment around this place tonight. Give my regards to the newlyweds. See ya."

As he walked away, I glanced over my shoulder at the couple in question. They were sitting beside each other sharing a cigarette and seeming quite content with themselves. No reason sprang to mind as to why they shouldn't be. 'Live and let live' and 'No harm, no foul' were two adages that occurred to me with regard to their previous antics. A refreshing sense of general tolerance towards people had invigorated my mood. I am usually much too critical.

And what fun is there in that? Yeah, I thought to myself, 'Live and let live!' If I could really start to apply that philosophy to my own life, it would be a wonderful fiftieth birthday present to myself. Tolerance is a virtue after all, is it not? Learning to be more tolerant of others might well teach me to be more tolerant of myself, and wouldn't that be a pleasant alteration of character. I'd just whipped a bar coaster through the air. No one arrested me. No one even criticized me. In fact, I got a free drink out of it and met an interesting person; a man with a far more troubled life than my own.

Obviously this guy's case was unusual. He may not live much longer. In fact, he may not *want* to live much longer.

―――

Yesterday, Friday, I was scheduled for a medical check-up at one of the major hospitals in Bangkok. It had been a few years since my last one, and I figured it would be a nice present to be given a clean bill of health on the eve of my transition from middle age to senior citizenship.

The appointment had been arranged on Monday when I met briefly with the doctor. He asked me how I felt and I said "fine" which, at the time, was true. He then said, "Well, your general appearance seems to be in order, so that's encouraging."

It concerned me for a moment that he hadn't said my general appearance looked good or looked healthy. He simply said that it "seems to be in order." In other words, my nose was pretty much centrally located between a pair of eyes and a mouth; an ear was attached on either side of my head; and two proportionally dimensioned arms and legs were positioned around the torso according to convention. I failed to appreciate what was especially encouraging about such an assessment of my general appearance. After all, the same could be said about most dead people.

The doc went on to recommend a series of medical tests he felt would be appropriate for an aging fossil such as myself, and it was agreed that I would show up at his office at seven o'clock Friday morning. As I was leaving, he handed me a small brown plastic cup with a screw-on cap.

"Please use this to provide us with a stool sample," he said.

"A stool sample?" I asked. Of course, I knew what he meant, but I was feeling playful. And besides, a stool is what I prefer to think of as something comfortable to sit upon while drinking mind-altering, intoxicant fluids.

Some words have too many meanings as far as I'm concerned. 'Gay' is another one, but let's not get into that.

"Yes," said the doc, "a stool sample. A bowel movement."

"Ah, a bowel movement. You mean you want me to piss into this little brown cup?"

"No, that would be a urine sample. We'll take care of that when you come in Friday morning."

"Isn't urine a bowel movement?"

"Urine comes from the bladder, sir. The bladder is an organ."

"Not a bowel?"

"No. Your intestines are bowels."

"Like the colon, for example."

"Exactly."

"So, you'd like me to move my colon into this little brown cup?"

"I would like you to deposit a portion of the contents of your colon into the cup, if it isn't too much trouble."

"Stools?"

"That's correct, sir."

"There are *stools* in my colon?"

"Yes, sir. And, in your case, possibly elsewhere, as well."

"Ha! *Touché* doctor. I'm only joking with you."

"I was hoping that's what you were doing. Otherwise, I'd have to refer you to a different department. Now, wake up early Friday morning, put some of your shit into that cup, and get your ass into my office at seven o'clock. . . . Okay?"

Yeah, I like a guy who can take a bit of the mickey and still hold his ground. I thought about asking him, if urine came from the bladder and the bladder was an organ, then would it be correct to refer to the penis as a 'pipe organ'? But that would have been stupid and, unless I've been sitting on a stool for too long, stupidity is not usually one of my dominant traits.

I walked out of his office clutching my little brown shit cup and stepped into an elevator. As everyone knows, there is something about being in an elevator that seems to prohibit speech. I've never seen a sign in an elevator that says, *"No Talking Allowed!"* but nevertheless, the minute people enter one of these vertical transports they immediately become mute. Why is that? It's as if everyone suddenly imagines himself as being in the espionage business.

I got on at the sixth floor and pressed the 'M' button for mezzanine. Even in a country like Thailand, most of these aluminum-plated buttons have been stamped with varying combinations of dimples in order to accommodate blind people. It's all well intentioned, of course, but how the hell does a blind person know when the elevator stops at the floor that the Braille-impregnated button designates? If there isn't an automated voice-over announcement saying, "And by the way, for you people who can't fucking see, this is the third floor," then what's the point?

As a rule, hospital elevators seem to be more than twice the size of normal ones. The reason for this is because only in hospitals do you have instances of people entering the elevator while they're lying down. It is true that the general appearance of some of these people certainly does not seem to be in order.

No horizontal passengers were aboard the carriage I entered. Everyone was standing. A few nurses, couple of interns looking like they hadn't slept in a week, a young school boy with his mother, a security person who obviously managed to dress himself and make it to his job without fully waking up, and an assortment of out-patients like myself. The doors closed as if upon a soundless tomb. Just for the hell of it, I said out loud, "If this thing is called an elevator, how come we're going *down*?"

Not one person laughed. But then, I reckon hospital elevator audiences are about as tough as you'll find anywhere. Anyway, that was Monday and I haven't been back to the hospital since. For some reason, shortly after arranging the check-up, I began to feel rather queasy. From Monday afternoon until the time I woke up at the ungodly hour of 5:30 Friday morning, my overall health had deteriorated progressively. First, my sinuses clogged up as if I'd been snorting molasses. Within 48 hours, my throat was ablaze, the lungs seemed to be operating at about thirty percent capacity, and I was spitting up globs of what looked like tainted oysters. By Thursday evening every bone, muscle, and sinew in my body ached, and as I looked in the mirror just before crash-landing on the bed that night, even certain features of my general appearance did not seem to be in order. Clearly, I was dreading the prospect that this scheduled medical examination was going to reveal one or more serious, if not life-threatening, ailments.

That prospect posed a dilemma for me, which I tossed and turned, grappling with, for much of what was a most uneasy slumber Thursday night.

On the one hand, I am a firm believer that human life is an extremely unfair ordeal. In fact, I don't mind going on record as saying that life is probably the most unfair thing ever to happen to me. On the other hand, considering death, my death . . . it alarms me that I'm so woefully unprepared for it, so frightened of it.

When I was a young university student, death was a tantalizing, sweet melancholic subject of contemplation; merely academic compared to the way I think of it now. I wrote an essay on death when I was 21 years old. Professor gave me an A+. "Very well done," he wrote across the top of the paper. "A thoughtful and comprehensive treatment of the subject."

I had never met a person who was dying. Never talked to anyone who was dying. I'd heard about people dying, but what did I know about it? Nothing! I knew nothing about what it's really like to come face to face with the prospect of my own death, or what the process of dying is like. Nothing. But, I got an A+ for a "thoughtful and comprehensive treatment of the subject." That's laughable as I think back on it.

Nevertheless, why am I so afraid?

God, a Supreme Being, a Universal Consciousness. . . . Yes, I believe in all the hokum. I believe in an immortal soul, believe in reincarnation. . . . Still, I'm afraid! I don't want to die, to pass on, whatever. Rather have a lot more people I know pass on before me. Maybe then I'd be more at ease with the whole idea. Everybody is going to die sooner or later. That's a certainty and thank God it is. It would be absolutely intolerable to think that I was going to die and some of my friends were not. I just want to be the last one to go. Let everyone else lead the way.

If I'm so afraid of dying, why do I engage in self-destructive behavior?

Now, there's a good question. I smoke cigarettes, drink booze, have wanton sex, etcetera. Why? Driving drunk on a motorbike. How many times have I done that? That's death-defying behavior. Okay, so I fear death, and yet, I defy it.

Would I want to live forever?

Belief in an immortal soul suggests that I am going to live forever whether I like it or not. Curiously (ironically), it is the prospect of eternal life that disturbs me even more than death. My mind can dwell on the prospect of death for lengthy periods of time. On the concept of eternity, my mind just snaps after a few seconds. Life everlasting? A life that just goes on and on and on without end . . . forever and ever and ever. . . . Oops, snap!

Wouldn't death be a welcome relief after a while? Is it not eternity that I fear more than I do death? Hence, the smoking, the drinking, whoring around . . . and driving drunk on a motorbike?

Now, having said all that, I found myself sitting on the toilet at 5:45 yesterday morning in an effort to discharge the contents of my colon so as to provide a sample stool or two, via the little brown cup, for whichever member of the hospital staff has the unenviable task of fiddling around with human excrement as a livelihood.

Unfortunately, by that point, the ongoing decline of my health during the week had also rendered me hopelessly constipated. After half an hour of fruitless (perhaps, an indelicate adjective to use in this context) exertion, I decided to scrap the appointment and went back to bed. I woke up four hours later feeling entirely refreshed, fit as a fiddle, and ready for lust.

The room lights dimmed once again, indicating that the play reading was about to resume. Act II, Scene I had Muffy and Brad sitting on stage very close to one another. . . .

"Oh, Brad darling, I don't know how I'd have gotten through the last few days without you."

"Muffy, my sweet, you've been so strong through this whole ordeal. You're a most remarkable woman. William would be so proud of you."

"Please, must we speak of William at a time like this. You, darling, are the strong one. My goodness! Three times this afternoon. You're an absolute stallion."

"You inspire me, muffin-buns."

"I love it when you call me that. Do you think Sheryl suspects anything?"

"Certainly not. In fact, she's barely stopped crying since the tragedy. The woman is a wreck."

"Well, honestly! What in God's name is she weepy-poohing about? It was my goddamn husband who leapt from the eighty-eighth floor with flames tongue-lashing his rear end."

"You're quite right, dear."

"Don't you think there have been times when I've felt like crying out?"

"Well, you've had a few outbursts this afternoon, muffin-buns."

"Oh, Brad darling . . . how you make me laugh. But, otherwise, I've been saving my tears for the TV interview tonight with Winny 'the Gutsucker' Jones."

"I know it's horrible to say, but thank God your little Billy has been crying most of the afternoon. Otherwise, Maria might have heard us. What luck he's still teething."

"Not entirely luck, dear. I took the precaution of hiding his gum-numbing cream before you came over."

"You're an amazing woman, muffin. What a clever mind!"

"These are trying times, darling, but I do my best. Like I said, your support has been so helpful. You're my staff."

"It's been my pleasure."

"And it's been *my* pleasure."

"Tongue-lashing flames . . ."

"Oh, darling . . ."

"Shall we?"

"Let's rehearse one more time. Now darling, we're all familiar with Winny Jones' determination to have her guests reveal the most intimate details of their lives."

"Yes, dear."

"Well, I want to manage to sidestep those sort of questions without, of course, seeming to be rude."

"That's going to be tricky."

"I know, I know . . . but after all, I've just lost my husband. I'm in deep mourning."

"You're grieving."

"Exactly. I'm grieving. That sounds more poignant than mourning."

"I think so. And, in fact, the whole nation is grieving. Estimates indicate that it was the largest single-day death toll to ever occur in this country. You, muffin, have the honor of speaking for all the grieving souls who have been victimized by this enormous tragedy."

"Oh Brad, you make me feel so special. I wish you could be there during the interview to hold me and give me strength."

"So do I dear, but you must admit that that might not look right."

"No, no I suppose not. You will be watching though, won't you?"

"Absolutely. I'll be glued to the screen transmitting all kinds of loving thoughts."

"Will Sheryl be there with you?"

"I'm sure she will."

"You'll do your best to ignore her, won't you, darling."

"Naturally, my dearest."

"You're so sweet."

"Okay, now let's focus on what the main reason is for Winny the Gutsucker's interest in your particular story."

"The phone conversation between William and I just before his death."

"Exactly. That's what makes your story prime-time."

"But there must have been others who spoke to their loved ones, or whatever you want to call them."

"Certainly there were. The point is that for some reason the network has chosen to interview you. What that reason is, is probably immaterial. You're the chosen one, and we must make sure that you make the most of it. There's no telling what could come of this. If you come across as likeable and engaging and smart and pretty and sincere and . . ."

"Please, Brad, let's try not to put too much pressure on me. I get the point."

"More interviews could follow. Trust me, muffin-buns, the public is going to love you."

"I could be a star."

"For sure! Who knows, you may even wind up with your own show."

"Or in the movies!"

"Yes."

"One thing, darling, is that I don't want to become one of those boring national spokespersons for the trendy cause of the day sort of thing."

"You mean like rallying and supporting other grieving relatives."

"Precisely. That would be so tiresome and, of course, there's no money in it."

"Certainly not. That's what becomes of people as a result of poor marketing."

"Marketing is your business, darling. I trust your judgment completely."

"All right then. Let's go over that last tear-jerking phone conversation you had with William. And remember, I think it's important that you not start crying too soon. That looks phony. You want to build up to it. Get Winny the Gutsucker and, hopefully, most of the viewing public to be on the verge of tears first."

"Right."

"So, Maria's informed you that William is on the phone, you pick up the extension and say . . ."

"I say, 'Oh, love of my life, what sweet joy to hear from you so unexpectedly.' And he says, 'Oh, honey-lambkins, I love you with all my heart. Please, please remember that as long as you live'."

"Good. That's very good. Did he really used to call you 'honey-lambkins'?"

"No. He used to call me either 'candy-loins' or simply, 'bitch'."

"Yes, well, I think we should go with honey-lambkins."

"I agree."

"And following this initial exchange of charming endearments—which you want to make plain was always the way you two greeted each other on the phone—then what?"

"Then William carried on further with how much he loved me to the point where I started thinking it was our anniversary or something which I had forgotten. But, I explain that I sensed a note of desperation in his voice, and that's when he tells me what's going on. I thereupon immediately hit the remote control switch on our super resolution, 35-inch color television with the quadraphonic, handcrafted teakwood surround-sound speakers and . . ."

"Perhaps you should dispense with all the luxurious details and simply say you turned on the TV. I mean, we don't want to confuse what it is we're trying to market here, right muffin-buns?"

"Oh, all right. But he was so proud of that damn TV."

"Yes, well, let's never mind about that during the interview. After all, it's his pride in you that we mean to convince the public of. They must be impressed with what a true blue faithful and loving wife you are."

"*Were*, you mean."

"Whatever. Now, let me see your pretty little chin start to quiver."

"Like this?"

"Yes, yes, that's perfect. Remember to do that a couple of times before the tears begin to well up in your eyes."

"It's important that the welling up process is apparent before the tears actually begin to flow, right?"

"Oh, absolutely. And remember, the cameras they have these days are extremely attuned to catching the most subtle visual nuances. There's no need to worry about over-acting."

"In other words, I should strive to be as natural as possible."

"As natural as you can contrive to be, yes. That's the secret to success in this image-conscious era."

"Didn't one of the great philosophers say that 'image is everything'?"

"Actually, it was a tennis player who got paid a great deal of money to say that. Our firm had the account and

I was part of the creative-writing team that came up with that slogan. It was one of our most popular."

"A creative-writing *team* came up with that slogan? 'Image is everything' only consists of three words for Christsakes, Brad. There's a subject, a verb, and an object. Which part of that was your creative contribution? The verb, perhaps?"

"Don't be sarcastic, dear. The creative process involved in the advertising business is much more complicated than most people realize."

"I'm sorry, darling. The advertising business is full of frustrated novelists and poets. That's what I keep hearing, and so it must be true."

"And as for 'image is everything,' truer words were never spoken. Not in our lifetime, anyway."

"You're right. Now, Brad darling, I really think I've got it all down. Let's not rehearse the spontaneity out of it. And I need to rest, don't you think? Winnie Jones and her crew will be here in less than three hours."

"No point in looking *too* rested, muffin-buns. After all, you're meant to have been grieving inconsolably for the past three days. You should appear to be severely traumatized."

"You think I still seem less than appropriately exhausted?"

"Is that little Billy screaming again?"

"Poor child. What a Godsend teeth are. Traumatize me one more time you horny stud-stallion."

"Step aside Secretariat!"

Another woman then came on stage, acknowledged the scattering of applause, and announced that if there were no objections,

Scene II of Act II would commence immediately. Several people took the occasion to order another round of libations but, all in all, there were no objections.

This scene had Brad and his wife Sheryl sitting together with Muffy on a stool a few feet away from them. They were all in possession of mobile phones. Brad's began ringing and he put it to his ear. . . .

"Hello."

"Brad, darling, is that you?"

"Ah . . . yes, this is Mr. Wilkins. Who is calling?"

"Mr. Wilkins, is it? Who the fuck do you think is calling, damn it!"

"Mrs. Wilkins is right here if you'd like to speak to her."

"I most certainly would not! But I get your point. Do you believe that wanton hussy, Winnie Jones? Why they chose me to interview instead of the many others who had last-minute phone conversations with their soon-to-be- dead loved ones was 'probably immaterial.' That's what you said, remember?"

"Ah-huh."

"Ah-huh my ass! How was I to know they'd managed to get a transcript of William's and my phone conversation? That's the reason they wanted to interview me. It was a set-up, pure and simple. Did you notice how she strung me along, let me go through just about everything you and I rehearsed, and then she plays the tape of our real conversation?"

"Ah-huh."

"I had my chin quivering and tears welling up in my eyes just perfectly, don't you think?"

"Ah-huh."

"And just at the point when the first precious little teardrop slipped out of its eye socket and down my cheek, that heartless bitch says, 'Before we go any further, perhaps our viewing audience would like to hear a bit of yours and William's actual conversation.' A *bit* of it, mind you . . . the bit about you and Sheryl, and the bit about me calling William a 'dickwad' and him calling me a 'whore.' It was the most embarrassing moment of my entire life. I must have looked absolutely frightful!"

"Ah-huh."

"Brad, damn you, if you say 'ah-huh' once more, I'm going to come over there, slap you upside the head, and kick your butt into next week. You understand me? I need you. Now, more than ever. I need your arms around me."

"How would you like my hands around your neck, you marriage-meddling tramp!"

"Sheryl?"

"Sheryl, darling, please don't get involved in this. Hang up that phone."

"Don't you 'Sheryl darling' me, you whore-mongering bastard! What do you mean, 'don't get involved in this'? This is our marriage that's been made a public mockery of. What. . . ? Like I shouldn't get involved in our goddamn marriage!"

"Sheryl, I'm sorry . . . really I am."

"Oh, shut up Muffy! In less than thirty minutes this evening you've managed to make a public mockery of my marriage, and ridicule one of the dearest men I've ever known."

"Thank you, darling. That's very sweet of you, but you know me, I'll get over it."

"I wasn't referring to you, Brad. I was referring to William, you ass."

"Oh."

"Maria, would you please tend to little Billy. His crying is driving me mad!"

"And that's another matter. Just imagine how embarrassing this is going to be for all our children."

"Don't you worry your pretty little head about my children, Sheryl. They'll be just fine. . . . It's in the glove compartment of the car, Maria. The red Mercedes XL 90 convertible with super all-weather radial tires, tan Cordoban leather interior with dual air-bags, small-screen color TV, surround-sound compact disc entertainment center, built-in seat massage, global positioning satellite hookup, hands-free cellphone, and . . ."

"Muffy!"

"Oh. Sorry, Brad."

"Brad, I can't listen to you two anymore. I'm so angry I could scream. Poor William must be turning in his grave."

"What do you mean, 'turning in his grave'? It'll probably be weeks before they find his body."

"Well, don't expect me to be at the funeral. I plan to continue mourning for him privately. And as for you Muffy, I hope that common decency will compel you to resist the temptation of appearing on any more television interview programs. In fact, I think it would be best for everyone involved, both living and dead, if you were to maintain the low profile that your moral character so richly deserves. Good-night!" (Sheryl switches off her phone with a flourish and exits the stage.)

"You must forgive her, Muffy, she's very upset."

"No shit."

"This couldn't have happened at a worse time for her. Dr. Kadison took her off the daily sedatives last week. You know, what with the pregnancy and all."

"Sheryl's pregnant?"

"I thought you knew."

"How the hell was I supposed to know? Nobody told me."

"Oh. Well, we just found out ourselves late last month."

"Any idea who the father is, Brad?"

"That's not funny, Muffy."

"Sorry, you stud-stallion. . . . Maria! Billy's still crying. Did you rub that shit on his gums or what. . . ? Damn that woman! Okay, give him a rubber nipple to suck on."

"Poor little Billy. I guess this is what Sheryl and I have to look forward to."

"It'll be a year and a half before you'll have to worry about it, Brad. . . . Well then, Maria, give him one of yours to suck on. I don't care. Just quiet him down for Christsakes."

(Brad clicks off his phone and walks from the stage.)

"Now, listen Brad, I need you. We must figure out a way to be together more often like we were this afternoon. Wouldn't that be nice. . .? Brad. . . ? Oh now, don't concern yourself that it has anything to do with love. I'm not expecting some sort of emotional commitment from you. It's just that I need to be held once in a while and, you know . . . Brad. . . ? Well, must I spell it out for you? Okay . . . I need to be F-U-C-K-E-D . . . Brad. . . ? Hello, hello? Ah, the bastard. . . . Maria, stop that moaning, damn it!"

And so ended Act II.

The crowd seemed to be warming to this little play reading. Maybe it was the booze. But even people who had missed Act I were laughing throughout Act II, and the overall applause was much louder.

As the actress playing Muffy left the stage, four seemingly high-ranking military personnel entered the bar. Actually, a couple of them may have been members of the police force. Eight years in Thailand and I still have trouble telling them apart. I suppose in a sense that means I've been lucky enough so far to avoid having to deal with any them. Such was not the case during my many years of residency in Chicago. On two occasions I spent a night as a guest in the local lock-ups. . . .

The first time I was charged with 'disorderly conduct' for the trivial offense of referring to a female police officer as a "cantankerous bitch." I can no longer remember exactly why I let loose that remark. There was definitely something about the woman's demeanor that annoyed me—but then, for the most part, cops have always annoyed me. Many of them are pathetically insecure characters who would otherwise have grown up to become respected criminals. There is no doubt in my mind that this particular female cop had often been referred to as a bitch. In fact, she was probably proud to be known as one. Some women are like that. My guess is that she took offense at being referred to as a *cantankerous* bitch. And that was for one of two reasons—she understood the meaning of the word, or she just didn't like the sound of it.

In any case, it was late at night in early December, and I was driving my old beaten-up, flaming red Plymouth Duster along North Halstead Street. In the car with me was a young woman I'd met that evening while drinking copious amounts of beer and playing a pinball machine in a bar on Division Street. It was one of those joints that were referred to back then as a 'singles bar.' The idea was that single young men and women would enter these bars alone, imbibe vast quantities of various intoxicating elixirs, and exit as loving couples. It rarely happened that way for me. I usually entered these bars single and sober and stumbled out several hours later drunk and beside myself. On this particular evening I got lucky—or so it seemed for a while anyway. I forget the girl's name, but she was very pretty. What she saw in me that evening remains a mystery. Perhaps she was impressed by my skills with the rubber-coated flippers. You keep the ball in play long enough, the points add up, and someone is bound to notice. She came over alone and stood behind me. Close enough so that I could smell her perfume and feel the body heat. Ten seconds later, the ball slid along a dormant flipper and drained down the hole. When the final score was tallied, five crisp sounds—like a judge's wooden gavel—echoed from the scoreboard.

"You're good," she said. "I like the way you move when you play. Mind if I buy you a beer?"

Talk about the 'good ol' days.' American women still had the confidence to flirt with a man, maybe offer to buy him a drink, and even enjoy a bit of casual sex without worrying about contracting a fatal disease. Nowadays, a man with designs on an American woman is as likely to end up in a courtroom as a bedroom.

I sold my five bonus games for a buck to a stranger and joined the girl at the bar. We took turns buying each other beers, and by midnight she'd invited me back to her apartment. While we were on our way in my car, a news bulletin piped up from the radio announcing that John Lennon had just been assassinated in New York City. That upset me and the girl said, "You can't turn left here." Too bad. I turned left anyway. There was no traffic. Five seconds later I heard a siren and saw the red light flashing in my rear-view mirror. Half an hour after that, I was crowded into a jail cell with at least thirty other male malcontents. I was the white guy in a black suede sport coat, gray flannel trousers, and tasseled loafers.

The cops might well have charged me with 'drunk and disorderly conduct.' I'd knocked down a dozen beers that night. As it was, they only charged me with 'disorderly conduct.' Actually, it was the male cop who made the arrest, put on the handcuffs, and wrote up the charge. The fact that he didn't compound the offense with a charge of drunkenness suggested to me that I wasn't the only person who thought his partner was a bitch. I took some consolation in that, while standing up all night trying not to take my eyes off the surrounding rabble. Most of them seemed pretty much at home in that jail cell. By the time I was released nine hours later, a few of my cellmates and I had become rather chummy. They were amused that "some high-class white honkey" would get busted for such a relatively minor offense.

When I appeared before the judge at ten o'clock that morning, he read out the charge and said, "How do you plead?" His name was O'Malley.

I said, "Guilty, Judge."

"You enjoy last nights' accommodations?" he asked.

"Oh you bet, Judge. Real homey," I said. "The room service was a bit lax, though."

"Well if you be plannin' to grace us again any time soon with your presence, I'll have the lads look into that matter for you. Otherwise, I suggest you mind your tongue with a tad more discretion when addressing members of our fine city's constabulary."

"Yes, sir."

"In that case, you're free to go. The charges will be removed from your record."

"Thank you very much, Judge." I was about to say, "Top o' the mornin' to you," but why press my luck?

As I turned to leave he said, "By the way, nice sport coat."

The imposing members of the Thai militia fanned out upon the premises. One entered the upstairs lounge where I was, and positioned himself behind a vacant table across from me and just to the right of the honeymooning Dutch couple. The bridegroom looked at me and rolled his eyes. Obviously an encore performance was going to be out of the question any time real soon. Trying to make the best of the situation however, I heard him ask the waitress for another bottle of champagne.

Turning to my left, I noticed four more people enter through the front door, where two members of the officer corps had stationed themselves. These four new entrants were, from my hawk-eye appraisal, three males and one female—two corpulent men in their mid- to late-sixties, and two alluringly well-tapered young escorts, approximately twenty years old each. As was soon apparent, they were, in fact, two couples. To their credit, neither of the elderly gentlemen was attired in brown clothing. Perhaps word had gotten out of the perils in play this evening at the Bamboo Bar for men who dared to venture forth in garments of a brown complexion. Nevertheless, I recognized one of these characters as the porcine-faced politician who was guilty of so many corrupt offenses against his own compatriots that he might well have been lined up in front of a wall and shot years ago—brown suit or no brown suit. In a most appropriate turn of fate, this character tripped on the second step up the stairs while making his way to the table. He didn't exactly fall flat on his face, but he stumbled just enough to lose a bit of it. One of the uniformed gents grabbed his elbow, and Willard C. Calhoun yelled out, "Steady as she goes, governor!" That brought a few chuckles, but not from the porcine-faced fellow and his entourage.

As this pair of odd couples had seated themselves, the waitress walked up the steps with a bottle of champagne, a silver ice bucket, and two long-stemmed crystal glasses. Somebody snapped their fingers and the waitress altered her course, placing the effervescent refreshment on the new arrivals' table. She popped the cork and was then dispatched with orders to requisition two more glasses.

"Excuse me, gentlemen," said the bridegroom, "but I believe that champagne belongs to us. We ordered it five minutes ago."

By this time the militia had taken possession of the bottle and a waitress was filling their glasses.

"Must be some mistake," the other elderly Thai gentleman suggested. "We ordered this bottle of champagne an hour ago. I'm sure yours is on the way."

Just as it seemed that the bridegroom was about to protest further, one of the generals, or whatever he was, approached the honeymoon couple's table and said something very quietly to the bridegroom.

That put an end to the dispute rather quickly.

Welcome to Thailand, pal, I thought to myself.

Two waitresses soon appeared on the scene. One carrying additional glasses for the swine party, and the second one carrying another bottle of champagne plus accoutrements for the Dutch honeymooners. Within five minutes, all three couples were fondling their respective mates.

I ordered a Jameson on the rocks and began to reminisce upon the circumstances of my second night in a Chicago-land jail. . . .

A squad car pulled me over at about 10:30 on a Tuesday night as I was on the way home from visiting my brother the foot doctor. He and his family live in a middle- to upper-middle-class suburb of Chicago called Slumberville. It's not a real exciting place to live, but white folks raise children there because it has good schools, very little crime, clean streets, and several parks. As I understand it, members of the Slumberville police force are not allowed to be residents of the town itself. I could be wrong about that, but so what? One thing for certain is that Slumberville cops don't spend much time on the job dodging bullets or tracking down violent criminals. It's probably fair to assume that issuing a few parking tickets every month or so is pretty much the extent of crime-fighting activity that these slugs get involved with. Why two of them suddenly felt compelled to pull me over that night I have no idea.

I was driving a five-year-old, navy-blue Cadillac sedan at the time, and although it wasn't exactly in mint condition, it clearly looked a lot better than the red Plymouth Duster. At first it occurred to me that perhaps I was guilty of a local moving violation. Nothing moved in Slumberville after 9:00 p.m.

The two cops got out of their car with the flashing red light on top. A high-powered beacon shone through my back window, lighting up the inside of my car like a flare bomb in a cubby-hole. One cop positioned himself beside the front passenger side window, and the other one loomed above me. I handed over my driver's license and asked what the problem was. That question was ignored.

"Please turn off the ignition and step out of the vehicle, sir."

They had me put my hands on the hood of the car and frisked me.

"Your vehicle emissions control exam date has expired," one of them said to me.

"Huh?"

"You are required by the State of Illinois to have your vehicle tested for emissions control every 12 months, sir."

"Yeah, so?"

"So, according to our records, this vehicle is three months past due."

"Okay," I said. "I'll get right on it first thing tomorrow morning. How's that?"

That, of course, wasn't good enough. They handcuffed me, slid me in the back seat of their squad car, and we drove to the police station. There, I was relieved of my wallet and Swiss pocket-knife, and fingerprinted. I couldn't believe it.

While wiping the black ink off my hands, I said to one of the cops, "Jesus, how do you treat serious criminals around this joint?"

"Failing to have your vehicle tested for emissions control *is* a serious offense."

"Oh really," I said. "Well, next time I'm in Slumberville, maybe I'll just hang out around the local high school, sell heroin, and rape a few of the cheerleaders."

"You'll be hanging around our jail tonight, and any more comments like that, wise-ass, could well keep you here for a lot longer. What's the pocket-knife for?"

"You mean the one with the bottle opener, can opener, nail file, little scissors, Phillips-head screwdriver, and three-inch blade? Oh, I just carry it around with me in case I ever get the urge to hijack a busload of school children. Always be prepared, I say. Right?"

I was thereupon none too ceremoniously dispatched for confinement in the one and only jail cell that Slumberville has to offer. Another white guy was asleep on a cot when I entered. God only knows what his offense was. Probably got caught walking his dog without a pooper-scooper or something. He was still asleep when my brother the foot doctor came to bail me out around dawn the next morning.

These experiences, although unpleasant, were at least instances where I found myself in the throes of action. That seems to have rarely happened to me since I moved to Asia. I'm a Phineas Fogg who never left the whist table. Maybe I'll die of old age and on my tombstone have it written, "*Around the Block in Eighty Years.*"

When a middle-aged man travels halfway around the world to settle himself for five years in a palm-thatched-roof bungalow alongside a quiet bay on an island in the Gulf of Siam, casual observers are apt to excite themselves with fanciful speculations. If the object of these speculations happens to be a rather reclusive sort of fellow who generally demonstrates a preference for his own company over others, then the speculative slant tends toward negative rumors. Nevertheless, the rumors floating around about me do add a certain *je ne sais quoi* to what, in reality, is a dreadfully ho-hum operation.

It's a pity that some of the rumors about me aren't true. Actually, none of the rumors about me that I'm familiar with are true. I'm not a criminal-at-large from America who absconded with a shitload of money peddling illegal drugs. I don't work for the CIA or the DEA. I'm not dying of an incurable disease, and I never killed anybody except, perhaps, by Oscar's Reading Gaol definition.

Personally, I'm rather partial to the rumors regarding the CIA connection and . . . well, that I may have murdered someone. I guess it's the romantic in me.

The point is, I'm woefully lacking action or, dare I say, some thread of a plot in my life.

I decided to walk outside to the hotel terrace along the river.

Noticing the old woman still sitting alone in the wheelchair sipping her sherry, I nodded. She raised her glass and, ever so suavely, nodded back.

Now there's a broad who's been around the block, I thought to myself.

The Chao Phraya River—the River of Kings. It was once the main thoroughfare of Bangkok. All the canals, known as *klongs*, which used to dovetail throughout this city, were fed from it. Back then, Bangkok was often referred to as the "Venice of the East." Most of the *klongs* have long since been drained of water, filled with cement, and paved into roads. The few that remain are nothing more than open sewers. Even the great river itself has become a fetid depository of toxic filth and discarded debris. Nevertheless, there is still an aura of romance about it. When the glaze of the moonlight shimmers upon the surface of this mighty chocolate-colored waterway and the dark silhouettes of barges full of teakwood and rice glide along in the tow of tugboats, one's imagination can fancy auras of a bygone era.

I, however, found myself inappropriately preoccupied with dislodging a bit of a peanut from between two of my teeth. This reminded me of the fact that last week I had bought myself an electric-powered automatic toothbrush. . . .

I've had trouble with bleeding gums lately, and my dentist said the condition was a result of poor brushing habits. It isn't that I don't brush often enough. The problem is, I brush improperly. The dentist said that if I continue to use sweeping horizontal strokes, my gums would soon recede to the point where my teeth will fall out. This was alarming news. "You must brush up and down, front and back," she instructed. Of course, I'd been hearing that for years, but no one had told me my teeth were going to fall out.

Anyway, as a sort of pre-birthday present to myself, I bought this automatic toothbrush. It vibrates at 7,500 rpm; soft bristles. Now, I actually look forward to brushing my teeth. It's fun. And, as it turned out, the toothbrush was the only birthday present I've received for being fifty years old.

So, there you have it. Fifty years old, I get a toothbrush for a birthday present, which I bought for myself, and brushing my teeth has become one of the highlights of my day. . . . Ol' man river just keeps on rollin' along.

At the Bamboo Bar

Funny thing, come to think of it, I almost didn't make it to fifty. . . .

I was standing on a chair yesterday morning while cleaning the windows in my apartment. They were wide open and I had to reach up and around to wipe the soot of Bangkok off the outside surfaces. I was using a white cotton hand towel. Unfortunately, in my zeal for cleanliness, I had mistakenly opted to wax the parquet floor prior to getting at the windows. As I stretched my reach by rising on the balls of my feet, the chair slipped backwards and I began to tumble forward . . . forward out the window, that is.

As a surge of panic gripped my gonads, I dropped the plastic bottle of sky-blue window cleaner, reached back, and caught hold of the aluminum extrusion framing just as my belly button cleared the outside ledge. It was one of those experiences when, as the saying goes, your whole life passes before your eyes. . . .

Fortunately I have a very good internal editor, so in my case the experience wasn't all that unpleasant. If I had been the whiskey and cola guy, however, I might have jumped right out. . . .

———

Next thing I knew, I was re-entering the Bamboo Bar.

A sudden burst of laughter from the near end of the bar compelled me to dispense these musings upon my own mortality. What a marvelous tonic for a weary soul laughter is.

I noticed another man sitting in the same spot once occupied by, speaking of weary souls, the whiskey and cola guy. Sompong was standing on the other side of the bar with a proud grin on his face. He caught my eye, gave the thumbs-up sign, and motioned me to join them.

I strolled over, having a pretty good idea what had precipitated the merriment.

"I told this man the monkey joke," said Sompong. "It worked well. He liked it."

"So I heard," I replied. "It's a great little joke, uh?"

"Ah, I loved it," said the man. "It's a mighty fine joke indeed, sir. Aye, and in no small part for being told with the economy of pacing it deserves. Sompong, your delivery was artfully rendered."

"Khun Mac . . . he told me this joke."

"Mac, is it? Might you be havin' a bit of the Irish in ya, sir?"

"Irish-American, for whatever that's worth," I said.

"Irish-American, is it? Well, praise the Lord. That, plus the monkey joke, is worth another healthy sample of whatever it is I can provide to fill your glass. The name's O'Leary—Sean O'Leary. Is 'Mac' the address your prefer?"

"It's enough to cover the subject, sure."

"Well, then, Mac it is. Sompong, a drink for our friend here. What's your pleasure, Mac?"

"Khun Mac is drinking Jameson tonight, Father Sean," said Sompong. "Same as you."

"Jameson is it? Then bless my soul, make it a double, Sompong. Neat, I presume, Mac?"

"On the rocks, actually, if you don't mind."

"Aye, of course. You're American-Irish. A double Jameson, *on the rocks*, Sompong . . . if you please."

"Sompong," I called out, "far be it from me to contradict the custom of a true Irishman. *Mai aow nam kaeng* . . . no ice."

"A double Jameson, Khun Mac," replied Sompong. "Neat, no *nam kaeng*."

"Yes, please. *Khawp khun khrap*, Sompong."

"You speak Thai? Good for you," Sean said. "How long have you been in this delightful country?"

"No, I speak very little Thai. I've been living in this country for nearly eight years. Been coming here, on and off, for twenty. And yet, for better or worse, as I say, I speak very little Thai. Maybe I should be ashamed of that."

"Maybe you should," he said. "But, for some reason, I suspect you're not. In fact, so far, you're a man who doesn't seem to be ashamed of anything about himself. That's a rare disposition. Even when I gave you the 'business' about being a Yank who pollutes Irish whiskey with ice cubes."

"Yeah?"

"You took it in stride and changed your order."

"So what? You're a *true* Irishman; you're buyin' and so I figure, what have I got to lose. Never drunk Jameson neat before. Fifty years old and it's nice to know there are still a few more tricks I can learn. Nothing wrong with that, I reckon. . . . By the way, did Sompong refer to you as *Father* Sean?"

"That he did, sir."

"You're a priest?"

"Yes, I am. But there's no need to stand on ceremony about it. Apparently Sompong has had some charitable involvement with the Catholic school a short walk away from here. He likes calling me 'Father.'"

"Thais can be very respectful. Especially with regard to matters of status. You here on holiday, Father."

"Aye, sweet Jesus. . . . Now, there's no need for you goin' on with the Father business, Mac. Please call me Sean . . . just plain Sean. As you said, it's enough to cover the subject."

"Well, all right. But I had eight years of Jesuits, and you'll be the first priest I ever got away without calling 'Father.'"

"Jesuits! You poor boy. There are priests and then there are Jesuits. The world's greatest educators, but I reckon you've suffered enough. 'Sean' it is now, you got that?"

"Got it. Nice to meet you, Sean."

Sompong set down two coasters on the bar and placed our fresh drinks upon them.

"What a night this is for you, my fine Irish-American friend. Your first Jameson served pure as mama's milk and your first priest you haven't called 'Father.' Here's to ya and may ya be in Heaven half an hour before the Devil knows you're dead."

"Cheers, Sean. Thanks. What brings you to the Land of Smiles?"

"I came here to play golf. Thailand's got some great courses, and the climate is nice this time of year."

"What is it about priests and golf? Nearly every priest I've known plays the game."

"Maybe it's a substitute for sex. You ever think about that?"

"Yeah, but the thought passed. There's more to it than that, isn't there?"

"Good for you, my lad. Yes, there is more to it. A bloke once asked me, 'Don't you ever worry that one day you're gonna wake up and realize that you've basically wasted your entire life because you've been here doing this instead of there doing that, or vice versa?' Told him I worry more about the day I *don't* wake up. That scares the bejesus out o' me. Otherwise, I think the older you get, the more likely you are to have second thoughts about how you've lived your life and how you might have lived it differently and, perhaps, better. But, regret is a very expensive emotion that I do not recommend spending a lot of time and energy on. Live each day the best you can, and then let it go. Why spend one moment second-guessing the way you spent another moment? And, never ever compare the value of your life to that of someone else's life. One of the great things about the game of golf is that it teaches you that. It's just you and the elements of Nature. Play your own game as best you can and don't worry too much about beating someone else. The real satisfaction comes from improving your own score. Betting, playing for money, rather spoils the purity of the game. . . . However, if golf is your livelihood then . . . well, a guy's got to eat, I guess. It's certainly not an easy way to make a living, but not a bad way to learn about living."

"So, for you, golf is a passion."

"Yes, you could say that."

"Like sex might be a passion for a man who hasn't taken a vow of chastity."

"Perhaps."

"Okay."

"Would it surprise you if I were to say that despite my vow of chastity, sex is also a passion of mine?"

"Not especially. You're human."

"How do you feel about homosexuality?"

"Would that include lesbians?"

"Of course."

"I have no quarrel with lesbians. I enjoy everything about sex that they do. In fact, sometimes I think of myself as a lesbian trapped in a man's body."

"Ah, Mac, you have an amusing mind. I admire that."

The lights began to flicker once again.

"What's that about?" asked Sean. "Don't tell me it's closing time already."

I explained to him about the play reading that had been going on, and that the final act was now to get underway. In one minute I summed up what had happened so far, and Act III Scene I began. . . .

(Six months later. Brad and Muffy are sitting very close together on stage.)

"What I don't understand, Brad, is how the government comes up with these numbers. Two hundred and fifty thousand dollars for 'pain and suffering' plus 50,000 dollars for each child. And, because William's insurance benefits totaled over a million dollars, the quarter million pain and suffering amount has been denied to me. That just doesn't seem fair. I mean, the black female janitor married to some crackhead pimp got the pain and suffering money plus 50,000 bucks for each one of her 13 children."

"Muffy, dear, I think, all things considered, the government's compensation plan is extremely generous. I mean, just think for a minute what kind of benefits you would have received if you'd been living in Bangladesh."

"Oh Brad, don't be ridiculous. I wouldn't be caught dead living in Bangladesh. What are you, nuts? Where is Bangladesh, anyway?"

"It's a small country somewhat adjacent to Northeast India."

"Is that the place that's constantly being ravaged by floods and hurricanes and famine and whatnot?"

"Yes."

"Well then, why in God's name would I be living there. You'd have to be out of your mind to live in a joint like that."

"I think you're missing my point, dear."

"Well, if your point is to make me feel better because I'm not a half-starved rice farmer up to my armpits in flood waters and being blown to bits by hundred-mile-an-hour winds, forget it. This is America, damn it. Just look out the window. . . . Honest to God, if I never see another American flag in my life, it won't be too soon."

"My point, dear, is that you should try to be grateful that you do live in America and that your government has demonstrated an extraordinary degree of generosity in dealing with the victims, such as yourself, of this horrible tragedy. Believe me, no other country in the world would have done anywhere near this much."

"But . . ."

"Muffin-buns . . ."

"Oh, Brad. . . . Do me, do me one more time, my stud-stallion."

(Room lights flicker for thirty seconds and then dim once again.)

ACT III Scene II

"Good God, I needed that."

"Feeling better, muffin-buns?"

"Much, thank you."

"That's my girl."

"So, how's the expectant mother these days?"

"Sheryl?"

"Are there others you're responsible for?"

"Ha ha. She's doing okay, thanks. Gets a bit cranky once in a while, but I guess that's to be expected. You know how it is."

"You think I was a cranky prego?"

"Well, William would say once in a while that . . ."

"William? Did he tell you I was a cranky bitch when I was pregnant."

"No, no dear. Not in so many words."

"What do you mean, 'Not in so many words'? 'Cranky bitch' is only two fucking words. Did that duckweed use the 'W' word?"

"Settle down, Muffy. William was always a gentleman. That's what Sheryl always says: 'William was a gentleman.'"

"Sheryl and William, William and Sheryl. Don't you ever wonder if those two didn't get it on? She's been burning the torch for William longer than I have. I'm surprised she hasn't applied for some pain and suffering money."

"Well . . ."

"No?"

"Actually, she did receive 100,000 dollars last week for what is being referred to as 'collateral pain and suffering trauma.'"

"You're joking."

"No. She wrote a personal letter to Jacob Weintrab, the so-called 'Tsar of the Pain and Suffering Relief Fund.'"

"Fancy a Jew being called the 'tsar' of something. Has he no pride? I'd like to know how much money he's getting paid for his troubles. Probably more than any of the victims I'll bet. More than me, that's for sure. The government doesn't give a damn about my pain and suffering."

"That's not true, dear."

"It most certainly is true. How much money am I getting for it? Zip! That's how much. Zippa-dee-do-dah . . . not one stinking dime."

"Let's not forget the 50,000 for each of your two children. That's something, isn't it?"

"Do you think that when little Billy grows up he's going to be happy that the US government considered his father's life to be worth a measly 50,000 bucks? Hell, that won't be enough to get him through one year of college. And, as for Sarah, at the rate she's been breaking tennis rackets since her father died, her fifty grand will be gone in a few years."

"This whole thing's been very hard on Sarah, hasn't it?"

"Yes. Of course it has. She loved her father and misses him very much."

"And you? You loved and miss him as well, don't you?"

"Sure . . . in my own way. But life goes on. It's amazing how resilient the human spirit is. It makes me feel selfish and guilty sometimes when I think about it."

"How do you mean?"

"Well, if it had been me. If I'd been the one who died, I'd want to believe that William would be spending the rest of his miserable life virtually catatonic in a state of inconsolable grief and gloom. If I looked up or down from wherever I was and saw him laughing or enjoying a game of golf or still cheering for those ridiculous Chicago Cubs, I think it would make me angry. That's very selfish of me, isn't it, Brad?"

"Yes, I suppose it is. But I admire your honesty. You're a good woman, Muffy. I think it would be disrespectful to William's memory to think otherwise. He had his passions—laughter, golf, those ridiculous Chicago Cubs. You can't begrudge the living their passions. For all we know, they may be the most important characteristic separating us from the non-living. And when I say 'the non-living' I don't just mean dead people."

"I understand."

"William would want you to be happy—to go on living. And, I believe, despite what you say, that you would want the same for him if the situation were reversed."

"I certainly wouldn't want him bonking the bejesus out of Sheryl. That's for damn sure. I don't suppose you would either."

"No, I certainly wouldn't."

"See, now I feel guilty. Guilty about being the survivor, guilty about having sex with you. . . . I hate feeling guilty."

"Then maybe you should stop doing those things that make you feel guilty."

"You mean, like living."

"No, the other thing."

"Oh. Well, do you feel guilty about it?"

"Muffy, I'm in the marketing business and I make a very good living at it. I can't afford to have a guilty conscience about anything. It would ruin my career."

"I guess the million-dollar death insurance plus the hundred grand for the children isn't so bad after all. It's all tax-free, too. Still got the house, the cars. . . . The country club has offered us a free lifetime membership. That was nice of them. Maybe *I'll* start playing golf, who knows."

"That's the spirit, muffin-buns."

"They've got some very cute caddies at the club."

"Muffy, you're an irrepressible tart."

"Or, as William so eloquently put it during his farewell voyage . . ."

(Brad and Muffy together.) "Whoorrre!"

The lights flickered, dimmed, and then brightened. Cast members all assembled at the stage, and most of the bar patrons cheered. Shortly thereafter, Sean and I resumed our conversation.

"I take it your passion for sex involves young men," I said.

"My passion for sex *involves* no one. It does, however, concern itself with, as you say, young men. I find Asian men very appealing."

"Priests have gotten themselves in trouble with that, haven't they?"

"Oh yes . . . as I did myself. I got in trouble not for having sex with young men, but for publicly advocating tolerance for homosexual relationships. The bishop wasn't amused. I wasn't exactly defrocked, but I was kicked out of the parish and forbidden to administer the sacraments. It was the worst thing that ever happened to me in my life, and yet I had no regrets for having said what I said. You asked me if golf was a passion and I said yes. But I'll tell you this, passions are the playthings of youth. They are toys. What's important in life is not to find what you *want* to do; what's important is to find something you *need* to do. I believe in the existence of a human soul . . . that portion of every being which is the eternal flame of God's love . . . the Divine Presence, if you will. It was, and is, my need to be in the service of tending to that Presence."

"Your need?"

"Yes. If you're lucky you will find something that you *need* to do with your life. Then you'll realize that need is a far more compelling and noble motivation for action than desire could ever be."

"But once you were banished from the parish, the opportunity to pursue your need was withdrawn. So you've resorted to joining the common herd's inclination of toying with passions. Your passion being the game of golf."

"Is that what you think, my friend?"

"Well, so it would seem. And . . . and . . ."

"And what?"

"And it would also seem that you somehow managed to secure a fairly generous severance arrangement . . . what they call in the business world, 'a golden parachute.' I mean, here you are in Bangkok at one of the most expensive and fashionable bars in the Eastern Hemisphere, drinking imported Irish whiskey, and tomorrow you'll probably be playing golf. For all I know, you may very well have a room here at the Oriental Hotel."

"Oh, not just a room, Mac. I have a suite."

"No!"

"Absolutely."

"Tell me it's in the Author's Wing and I'm going to scream."

He reached out his hand, placed it across my mouth and said, "The Noel Coward Suite."

"Mother of mercy," he gasped as I gently clasped my teeth upon one of his fingers, "can this be the end of Rico!"

Okay, so the padre is familiar with American gangster films. That's the classic closing line of Edward G. Robinson from a 1930s film called *Little Caesar* . . . never mind.

The Author's Wing at the Oriental Hotel is located in the original building constructed more than 125 years ago. It now consists of four spacious and luxurious suites, each named for a famous writer who famously ensconced himself at this hotel whenever his good fortune brought him to the City of Angels in the Land of Smiles. These four gentlemen may not be your favorite writers, their critical acclaim is mixed. The first was a native Pole, two were English—as English as you could get in their time—and the baby of the brood was an American. They all wrote in English—even the American. All of them have been dead for quite a while. Some, of course, longer than others. They were all popular in their day, as far as I know. Curiously enough, death has enhanced only one of their reputations—the Polack. Nevertheless, there were four suites that needed naming and the honors are well deserved—Joseph Conrad, Somerset Maugham, Noel Coward, and James Michener. I think Coward was the most multi-talented of the four, and clearly one of the most stylish *bon vivants* who ever lived.

"The Noel Coward Suite! Well, I'll be damned," I said.

"The Good Lord works in mysterious ways."

"So I've heard, Sean, so I've heard."

"Would you be interested in hearing the particular mysterious way in which the Good Lord worked on my behalf?"

"Very much so."

"Then knock back your whiskey and we'll get out of here," he said. "Sompong, my bill, if you please."

"Where are you taking me, you evil man?"

"Someplace that might better inspire the raconteur in me. You ready?"

"I was born ready."

"I'll bet you were. Let's mosey along."

I had Sompong hold my tab for me, and the padre and I walked out the glass doors. We turned left in the aisle and headed towards the lobby.

"Wait a minute, my lad. How about a cigar?"

"Jesus, this story needs a cigar?"

"Aye, it wouldn't be hurtin' the cause none. You like cigars?"

"Not especially," I said.

"You ever had the best money could buy?"

"I've never had the best of anything money could buy, far as I know."

"Well let's see if we can't do something about that, bein' as this is your fiftieth birthday. Follow me."

We turned around and entered a cigar shop situated right next to the Bamboo Bar. The proper name for such a place is . . . is . . . well, a 'tobacconist' or 'tobacconary' or something like that. In any case, the joint reeked of tobacco, that was for sure. It was called La Casa del Habano. I've never been much of a cigar smoker, but I know that the Cuban varieties are reputed to be the best in the world. They have been unavailable in the United States for most of my lifetime due to the unfriendly nature of Cuba's corrupt dictatorial regime. It's not that the US has any objection to doing business with corrupt dictatorships, but we do prefer them to be friendly. If they're not going to be friendly, then they better have something a bit more valuable to offer than cigars. Oil, for example, would be nice.

Sean explained that Cohiba are the best of the Cuban cigar brands. They come in various sizes, and he bought half a dozen of the longest and fattest called Churchills. They cost about fifty dollars apiece, which according to him was a bargain. The Coronas Especiales were of a more appealing size to me, so Sean bought two of them, as well as a couple of Esplendidos.

From there we walked across the lobby and along a narrow passageway lined by a glassed-in atrium on the left, and several fancy boutiques on the right. This led us to the original building of the hotel. On the ground floor is the Lord Jim Room where tea is served every afternoon. A dual staircase leads up to the private floor where the four Author's Suites are located. We walked to the right at the top of the stairs and then left down a short hallway. And there it was—the Noel Coward Suite. I noticed a wooden matchstick propped up against the base of the door.

"That lets the hotel staff know that the guest is out of the room. Then they come in and tidy things up," Sean explained.

"A wooden matchstick?" I said rather incredulously. "Doesn't that seem kind of tacky for a hotel of this stature?"

"Well, you could look at it that way if you like," he said. "Or, you could think, as I prefer to do, that this is the custom that was used in the old days. That way it makes it seem rather charming."

"*Is* this the way they used to do it in the old days?"

"Frankly, I have no idea. I haven't asked."

"But you prefer to think they did."

"That's correct."

"I see."

"Any other critical observations you'd like to make before we enter the suite?"

I replied that there weren't any which sprung to mind. He said that was nice to hear, and so we entered the suite. My first general impression was of being awash in the cooling colors of blues and greens. Then it was all the silken fabrics and the teakwood and the gold-painted, hand-wrought carvings that flooded into view. Strangely enough, the first object I managed to focus upon specifically was a silver-framed photograph of the great man himself, which rested on a small table beside the sofa. A puffy-faced Noel Coward, eyebrows arched above the rim of black sunglasses, a cigarette looking very much at home between the middle and ring finger of his right hand. . . . He was wearing an open-necked, bright-colored floral shirt and a slightly down-turned mischievous grin that seemed to be savoring a few clever *bon mots* that were on the verge of being released in a cloud of smoke.

Sean opened the teakwood liquor cabinet, put together a couple of Jameson's on the rocks, and proceeded to give me a tour of the joint. The suite is basically a three-room affair—the front room that you first enter, the bedroom, and then a bathroom. The walls of the bedroom are paneled in silk designed with little flame-like patterns rising to the ceiling. The two four-poster, canopied, single beds are the main features. There are a couple of chairs, a small table in front of a large rectangular mirror in a gold-painted, intricately carved frame, lots of French-blue silk cushions, a ceiling fan, soft green carpet, a bowl of fruit, a vase of orchids and, of course, a television.

A moderate size, marble-floored, wood-paneled dressing room adjoins the bedroom and bathroom. In hotel parlance, that is known as having a bathroom *en suite*. And, at a cost of approximately 1,200 dollars a night, I suppose that it's only fair that guests should not have to share a communal toilet down the hall or step out into the garden to relieve their bowels. That sort of procedure may have been *de rigueur* back in the early days of the hotel 125 years ago, but then the Oriental was known as a "seafarers lodge," the room rates were 75 cents a night and, incredible as it may seem, the accommodations were so basic they didn't even include a television. It's a wonder how people managed to survive back in those days.

The bathroom itself was, to my mind, the sexiest and most appealing room of the lot. Try to ignore whatever reflections you may have with regard to the sort of mind I may possess which that statement arouses. Black and white marble floor; grand, old fashioned porcelain tub supported by four gold-plated iron feet; glass-enclosed shower; sparkling, gold-framed mirrors; thick, fluffy white towels; a ceramic bowl of floating jasmine buds; and sliding, hand-carved gold doors that could well provide a view from the dressing room to delight even the most veteran of voyeurs . . . or—and I hadn't thought about this until just now—a similarly enticing view from the other way around.

We retreated into the front room where I made myself comfortable on the sofa beside the photograph of Noel Coward. Sean opened a window that overlooked a small green lawn bordered by palm trees. The sweet scent of frangipani wafted into the room—without a doubt, one of the most enchanting fragrances of Southeast Asia. In the background were the sounds of longtail boat taxis and cargo-hauling barges going about their business along the Chao Phraya River.

Sean clipped the ends off two cigars and passed one to me. We lit them and we puffed. After a moment he said, "Well, how do you like it?"

"Compared to what?" I replied.

"Never mind compared to what, you silly lad. You're fifty years old. It's about time you began to appreciate things without making comparisons. In fact, as far as the finer things in life are concerned, it's the only real way to appreciate them."

"All right. I like it. Very flavorful. Not like anything I've had before."

"Exactly."

"You supposed to inhale these things?"

"You're supposed to *enjoy* them. Sometimes I inhale a little bit, but you don't have to."

"So," I said, "God's mysterious ways. . . ."

"Right. Well, this is what happened. . . . Needless to say, I was extremely depressed after the bishop had me removed from the parish. I drank quite a bit. I drank quite a bit for quite a few days, in fact. I really had no idea what to do with myself. But, I kept praying. Despite all the booze, I kept praying because I never lost my faith. Then one evening several members of the parish invited me out to dinner. A married couple and a widower about my age. The three of them had been very supportive, and over the years had become good friends. They knew how upset I was, and so they dragged me off to a local pub to try and cheer me up some. It was on a Friday night and we all got pretty drunk. Now these three people all had the habit of buying lottery tickets once a week. That sort of thing never made a lot of sense to me. I'll wager on the horses or a golf game once in a while, but Ireland's lottery just seemed like a waste of money. I suppose it's the same with lotteries everywhere. People spend a few quid, and for a week it gives them license to a fantasy . . . a fantasy that somehow distracts them from the dreary, mundane routines of their daily lives. Me, I never felt the need for that kind of ruse. I enjoyed my daily routine."

"You had a mission."

"Yes. It's been my greatest blessing. Anyway, that night, I'm not sure how it happened, but these people talked me into putting up some money for the next week's draw. Apparently there hadn't been a winning ticket for over a month, so the jackpot just kept growing. The four of us each chipped in ten quid, and to tell you the truth, by the next day I'd completely forgotten about it. Well, sure enough, the following Thursday night I got a phone call from Brendan. He's the widower. We won the bloody lottery . . . 16 million punts—four million apiece."

"My God!"

"That's precisely what I said."

"I'll bet the Jameson was flowing in buckets *that* night."

"It may well have been, but not down my throat. I went straight over to the church, closed myself into an empty confessional box, and just knelt there for hours. Finally fell asleep stretched out on a back pew. Woke up the next morning, went straight to a travel agent, and ten days later I landed in Bombay. It was only on a whim that I went there."

"Or, one of God's mysterious ways, perhaps."

"Yes. I'm sure you're right. Saw more poverty on the ride into town from the airport than I'd ever seen in my entire life. It was exactly the place I needed to be at the time. After making some general inquiries during my first few days there, I heard about a Christian orphanage about 150 miles southeast of Bombay. The place was a shambles. It was struggling to care for and educate 22 children. Now, three years later, it's been completely re-built and tends to the needs of nearly 200 orphaned children. Christians, Hindus, Muslims—they're all welcome. We try not to favor one religion over another. When I'm there, I say Mass every day, and anybody who wants to attend is free to do so. Otherwise, the only sort of remotely religious doctrine that we make an effort to instill in these children is the good 'ol golden rule . . . namely, treat others as you would have them treat yourself."

"I suppose if all people practiced that one, it wouldn't make much difference what their religion was."

"Yeah, that's pretty much the way I figure it. . . . You gettin' on with that cigar all right?"

"Not bad. But it would be an expensive habit for me."

"Well, buy a lottery ticket tomorrow. Maybe you'll get lucky."

"Better I should give you the money and you buy it for me."

"Ha."

"This orphanage project must have cost you a good deal of money, huh?"

"Aye, but that was of no concern to me," he said. "What's the price of a smile? What's it worth? Should there be a market place where smiles can be bought and sold, same as there is for soybeans and pork bellies? Where is the market place for love and joy and laughter and kindness and tolerance? Are these negotiable commodities? Should they only be given away, or do they have an exchange value? Who would trade me what for a smile?"

Good Lord, I thought, it had been a long time since I'd heard anyone answer a question that well without ever making a declarative statement. The only appropriate response I could think of at that moment was to raise my glass in salute.

"Amen," he said.

After a brief pause, I asked, "So, you spend most of your time in India these days?"

"No. See, now we're getting to the 'God's mysterious ways' part of the story."

"Oh?"

"Yeah. Year and a half ago an article appeared in *The Times* about this banished, renegade priest from Ireland who had gone and done some good in India. Few more stories followed that one, and lo and behold I got word that the bishop wanted to see me. Seems he'd gotten a call from Rome. I like to think that maybe he got a call from God, as well. In any case, he couldn't have been nicer. He commended me on the project with the orphanage. That I kind of expected. But then, he actually apologized to me—said he was wrong for what he'd done and asked me to forgive him."

"Did you?"

"Of course."

"*Do* you?"

"Why not? It's a lot easier to forgive than it is to hold a grudge."

"Ah, the Golden Rule . . ."

"Or, 'Please forgive us our trespasses as we forgive those who trespass against us.'"

"That's a good one."

"It is, indeed," he agreed.

"How about, 'Lead us into temptation but deliver us from evil.' I like that one, too."

"Yeah well, your wording is a little off there, but nice try."

"If you don't mind my asking, how do you deal with sex?"

"I deal without it."

"Met a guy once, claimed he wanked off first thing every morning. Said it relieved the pressure and allowed him to focus on more important things during the rest of the day."

"Wanked off every morning, did he?"

"First thing. Right out of the gate. So he claimed."

"Was that before or after saying Mass and receiving Communion with the body and blood of Christ?"

"As you do?"

"Every morning."

"Right out of the gate?"

"Pretty much so."

"Well, this guy wasn't a priest."

"You don't say."

"No. He was as an Aussie."

"What a surprise."

We sat there for a moment or two without speaking. It's unusual for me to be comfortable doing that with someone who I've only known for a short period of time. He was enjoying his cigar. I was simply enjoying the ambience of the Noel Coward Suite, listening to the crickets, the palms dancing with the breeze, little waves splashing against the embankment beside the hotel terrace . . . and I found myself wishing I were alone.

"You look like a man lost in a reverie," said Sean.

"Right."

"Of what?"

"Of a bygone era," I said.

"Know exactly what you mean. I get that way myself around here once in a while. Friendly ghosts having a bit of fun with us, maybe."

"I'm all for friendly ghosts," I said.

"Blithe spirits . . . like our host in the silver frame beside you."

"Ha. Indeed."

"Another drink, my boy?"

"Yeah, but down in the bar. I'm starting to get a bit too cozy here. One more drink and I might kick you out."

He laughed at that and said he'd be down a little later. I said don't forget about the wooden matchstick.

———

When I got back to the Bamboo Bar, it must have been around midnight. You could say my birthday was just about officially over. But that wasn't the way I figured it. Considering the fact that I was born in Chicago, and that Chicago time was 13 hours behind Bangkok, I reckoned there was still plenty of time left to celebrate. Catching Sompong's attention, I raised my right index finger and he had a fresh whiskey waiting for me by the time I got to the bar. It was a double, neat.

"Father Sean called five minutes ago and said have this ready for you. It's on him."

Clearly the world would be a better place if there were more priests like Father Sean hanging about the premises.

"You don't want ice with this, do you?" asked Sompong.

"Hell no," I replied. "Whiskey neat for the rest of the night, pal. I've been converted."

"Good. Father Sean said I should charge you ten dollars if you ask for ice. He's a very funny man, Father Sean."

"That he is. To Father Sean. . . . Cheers, Sompong."

Just then I took cognizance of the fact that a lady sitting two stools away had been stirring her mug of Irish coffee for several minutes. Metal spoon clanging around the glass mug. What an annoying racket! Why do people do that? You'd think this woman was drilling for oil or something. I had a girlfriend once who used to do that. She said it was "therapeutic."

"What, like it helps calm your nerves, you mean?" I had asked.

"Yes, something like that," she said.

"Well, it's frazzling the shit out of my nerves. Why don't you stop?"

"Okay," she said. "Here, you try it for a while."

That girl and I never did communicate very well. I called her 'Purgatory.'

Sompong sidled along behind the bar, placed a glass of pink champagne in front of me, and handed me a note.

"This is from the gentleman at the corner table, Mr. Mac." He nodded towards the front of the room over my left shoulder. The note read: *"Don't shoot! If you'd like some of the real stuff, please join us."*

I turned around and spotted Willard C. Calhoun waving a white cloth. He and Betsy-May were sitting at the table previously occupied by the old woman in the wheelchair. Previously occupied *alone*, that is, by the old woman in the wheelchair. She was still there and, needless to say I suppose, still in the same seat.

As I reached their table, I wagged a finger at the now familiar white cotton cloth and said, "Well you ol' kleptomaniac. I see you went back and nabbed one of those fancy little towelettes."

"Two of 'em, actually," said Willard. "But it wasn't me. Betsy-May did it. Got 'em in the ladies room, as well. How 'bout that!"

"Oh hush up, you big bear," said Betsy-May. "Mac, meet our new dear friend here. This is Mrs. Genevieve Langdon. Genevieve, this is Mac."

"Mrs. Langdon," I said, "how do you do" or "nice to meet you" or something like that. I knew instinctively from just looking at her that she was one of those grand old dames who had been raised in an era before men and women shook hands upon meeting each other. Having been raised myself, to an extent, at the very end of that era, I still, to this day, never initiate the modern custom of shaking a woman's hand. Funny, huh?

"Mac," she said, "it is a pleasure to make your acquaintance." She elegantly extended her right hand, palm down, just as I expected her to do. I clasped it gently and she said, "Please, call me Genevieve."

"The pleasure is mine."

"You'll forgive me for not getting up, Mac? I've only one leg to stand on these days."

"Madam," I said, "something tells me that even with two legs there was never a man you got up from a chair to meet."

"Quite right you are, sir. Now, quit standing on ceremony and sit down with us. Please."

She was what one might describe as a full-bodied woman. Excepting, of course, that she was missing a notable appendage. A black silk dress with randomly spaced mauve diagonal stripes and slightly flared sleeves . . . sunflower yellow Kashmiri scarf draping the shoulders . . . diamond and red garnet earrings . . . hair the color of a fingernail moon peeping out the side of a fluffy midnight cloud pulled back against a high brow creased by age, curiosity, the resultant wisdom, and God knows what else . . . a buxom, pearly bosom gently ebbed and flowed in the low-cut silken cleavage of her dress with every breath of air she graced and . . . and, well, an aura about her to which you just hoped she could give a voice. When she said, "Now, quit standing on ceremony and sit down with us. Please," I complied without hesitation, which was a good sign.

"Where you been?" asked Willard. "We thought maybe you'd cashed in your chips for the night. We asked the bartender—what's his name?"

"Sompong."

"Yeah, right. We asked him about you and he said you'd gone off with an Irish priest. One a' them Irish Catholic priests. You all right, Mac?"

"Far as I know, yeah. Why shouldn't I be?"

"Pay no mind to him, Mac," said Betsy-May. "My ol' Willard had his fill of Irish Catholic priests when he was a youngster. But, believe you me, I reckon they had their fill of Willard, too. He was a real hell-raiser in his early days."

"Now, sugar-plum."

"Willard, the truth be known, those priests probably kept you outta a lot of trouble you otherwise would have gotten into. It's a wonder your dear ol' momma didn't have a nervous breakdown what with all the mischief you and your brothers stirred up."

"Well, alls I can say is them Japs in the POW camp weren't much worse than the priests I had to put up with as a kid."

"Oh honestly, Willard."

"Now, now, my darlings," said Genevieve. "Shall we offer Mac some of the bubbly? I understand you're fifty years old this evening. That would make you, if I'm not being too presumptuous, the baby of our little party here. Dom Perignon suit you, young man?"

"Suits me just fine," I said.

As Willard started to reach for the bottle, Genevieve said, "Allow me, my dear man. When it comes to pouring champagne . . . well, it's one of the few dexterities I still have a talent for."

She gently removed the bottle from the ice bucket, slowly pulling it along the sterling silver rim in order to drain the water off it, tilted the crystal glass, and rather insinuated the champagne into it. She made a sort of artful ceremony out of the process. Much like the way the bartender at O'Rourke's used to draw Guinness.

Handing me the glass she said, "*A votre sante* and happy birthday."

"*A votre sante, aussi et merci beaucoup*, madam."

The champagne tasted marvelous.

"*Parlez vous Français, monsieur?*" she asked.

"No," I said. "Still working on English. Fifty years at it and I continue to learn."

"Well, you know the old saying, Mac, if you speak two languages you're bi-lingual, if you speak three languages you're tri-lingual, and if you speak one language you're American."

"Yeah, I've heard that one before. Fairly understandable, though. America's a big country. State of Michigan alone is as big as Great Britain. If they spoke different languages in Illinois and Wisconsin and Ohio, I'm sure Americans would be just as multi-lingual as the Europeans are."

"Betsy-May and I is multi-langual, ain't we sugar-plum? We speaks English and hillbilly, so there."

"Oh, by the way, Mac," said Betsy-May, "those four people who came in earlier with all the bodyguards or whatever they were. . . . You reckon the young people were children of the two elderly Thai men? Willard and I couldn't figure that out."

"Well, judging from the action that was going on under their table," I replied, "it would seem to me that their relationships are of another nature."

"Golly me," whispered Betsy-May. "Of another nature indeed, if you want my opinion. The one man had his hand on that boy's lap. I noticed that when I was walking around the room."

"Snooping around the room is more like it," said Willard.

"Now that's not true, darn it. But, I mean, honest to goodness!"

"Now, now, sugar-plum, don't be gettin' your knickers all tied up in a knot. This is a free country here, and that boy is certainly old enough to know what he wants. Same with the young woman. And on that note, I'm gonna excuse myself and retire to the men's laboratory to experiment on myself. Ha! Oh gosh, I apologize, but this here champagne. . . . Sugar-plum, I'll be back a better man. You just trust me."

In a moment he was gone.

Betsy-May was about to say something but Genevieve beat her to the punch:

"Never apologize for your man, dear. I learned that early on in my life, and it's lesson that's kept many romances alive that might otherwise have wilted from over-exposure."

"That's probably good advice, Genevieve. Unlike myself, I'm sure you've had a great many . . . ah . . ."

"Shall we say 'exposures,' dear?"

"Ha. You see, Willard has been my only exposure to romance. He's the romance of my life. My first, my one and only. And, believe you me, I'm certainly not apologizing for *that*. We've been very blessed."

"Indeed you have, my dear. Every woman hopes that her first will be her last . . . her one and only. I know I did. But, when that man ups and dies on you . . . well, what's a woman to do?

I lit a cigarette.

"This is probably boring you, Mac? Two elderly matrons talking of love," Genevieve said to me.

"No, not at all. I just thought I'd light up a smoke and settle in to listen."

"You are a true gentleman, sir."

"I was rather wondering though . . . I mean. . . . Oh, never mind."

"No, no . . . speak up. After all, it's your birthday. What were you wondering about?"

"Well, if it isn't just a coincidence that you happen to have the same name as the one on the board in the lobby, I assume you're the Genevieve Langdon who wrote the little play that was given a reading here tonight, right?"

"Oh, she's the one," said Betsy-May. "Wasn't it just a stitch! Willard and I haven't laughed so hard in a coon's age."

"Go on, Mac. You were wondering. . . ?"

"I was wondering that with all your talk about love and romance a moment ago . . . well, the characters in your play seemed to be rather lacking in their allegiance to the virtues of romantic love, if that's the way to put it."

"A most astute observation, Mac. Carry on."

"May I have some more champagne first?"

"Of course you may, and allow me."

Genevieve ever so gracefully decanted what was left of the bottle into my glass, motioned a waitress over to our table, and ordered another Dom Perignon.

I had noticed before . . . the frosted contours of the lithe female form on the outside surface of the champagne glass . . . a female form similar in age and innocence to a David Hamilton photograph. Raising the glass towards Genevieve in an *a salude* manner I remarked, "This is Lalique crystal."

"My goodness. Yet another astute observation. Betsy-May, I fear we are in the company of a gentleman whose sophistication may be more challenging than we are worthy of appreciating."

"They're your glasses, I assume."

"Four champagne flutes, four brandy snifters, and two sherry glasses. Yes, they're Lalique. I never travel without them."

"It's my favorite crystal," I said. "Why four champagne flutes, four brandy snifters, but only two sherry glasses?"

"I have a feeling you'll find out about that later," she said. "As for now, it looks as if it's going to be a photo-finish in the race to our table between Willard and the pretty young lady with our next bottle of champagne."

She was right. They both arrived at exactly the same time . . . fortunately without running into each other. Willard was in an obvious state of restrained agitation, much like the cork being slowly twisted from the neck of the Dom Perignon. They nearly popped off with the same synchronization as they had in arriving at their present destination. Willard's cork was twisted off by his wife saying in a tone of guarded sympathy, "Oh darling, not again?"

"Three ways this time," he replied sullenly as Genevieve performed a champagne transfusion to the four frosted maidens. Thoughts of Keats' "Ode on a Grecian Urn" came to mind but were rapidly short-circuited from "Thou still unravish'd bride of quietness, Thou foster child of silence and slow time," to "When old age shall this generation waste, thou shalt remain, in midst of other woe than ours . . ."

"I mean, split in two was bad enough," continued Willard. "Now it went in three directions . . . all over the damn place. Hell, who knows, in half an hour maybe I'll be able to stand up here at the table and refill all our glasses myself. Save us some money anyway, wouldn't it?"

"Now Willard, darling, just settle yourself down. Genevieve, Mac, I'm sorry . . ."

"Dear. . . ?"

"Oh right, Genevieve. Okay, I'm not apologizing. Willard, since you've brought this whole matter up, we might just as well explain the situation. Shall we. . . ? Willard . . . are you there?"

"Oh all right," he said. "Go ahead, tell them. I'm sure it's just the subject they've been dyin' to discuss all evening."

"Willard has a slight problem with his prostrate gland," Betsy-May said sheepishly.

"*Prostate* gland," corrected Genevieve.

"Say what?"

"It's called the *prostate* gland, dear. Not *prostrate*."

"Oh?"

"Prostrate is the name of a position one is in while lying down. It's a gender-neutral bit of terminology. Prostate, on the other hand, is the name of the gland, peculiar to humans of a male persuasion, such as Willard, for example. And, of course, not to ignore our birthday boy, Mac, as well."

"Well, in any case," Betsy-May continued, "Willard has a slight problem with it. 'Slight problem,' if I may remind you dear, is exactly the phrase Dr. Murray used to describe it. 'Very common in men of your age, and nothing to be terribly concerned about at this stage,' he said."

"That was at the double split-stream stage, darlin'. Now I'm suddenly at the triple split-stream stage." Willard drained his glass of champagne in one gulp and said, "This bottle's on me. Fill 'er up please, Genevieve."

"Was the flow interrupted at all, dear?" asked Betsy-May. "That's important to watch for," she explained to us. "An interrupted flow during urination is also a sign of trouble."

"Well, I'm not sure," said Willard. "I couldn't really keep my eyes on all three of them at the same time."

Genevieve was sitting directly across the table from Willard. She held up three fingers and said, "Quickly now Willard, how many fingers am I holding up?"

"Three," he said.

Genevieve immediately put her hand back down on the table and said, "Just as I suspected. Have another glass of champagne. I was only holding up two fingers, you silly dear."

"Nonsense!" said Willard. "I swear you were holding up three fingers. That's what I saw . . . three fingers."

"I'll thank you not to swear at me, sir. I know how many fingers I was holding up. Two, that's how many. Betsy-May, Mac, how many fingers was I holding up?"

"Two," we both said.

"Now, there you have it. Confirmation from a couple of God's most stellar witnesses. I have no doubt that you may have seen three fingers and three amber rivulets as well, but it's been a long evening. The fact of the matter is, you may have more of a problem with your eyesight than you do with your prostate gland. Skip the proctologist and visit an optometrist when you get back home. Now, enough of this silliness. Betsy-May, Mac, your glasses please. Time we started to catch up with Mr. Magoo here."

"Well, by golly, I never thought about that. Maybe you're right, Genevieve. Sugar, was she really holding up only two fingers?"

"Would I lie to you, you love of my life?"

"Gosh, I feel much better now." He raised his glass and said, "Cheers to the world!"

We all joined in on that one, and then Genevieve proceeded to say, "Now Willard, while you were off in the men's room becoming distraught over the condition of your prostate gland, Betsy-May and I were engaged in a discussion of a different although, perhaps, not entirely unrelated matter."

"Oh, sugar-plum, you weren't talking about the lump on your breast were you?"

"No, Willard, I most certainly was not! How very thoughtful of you to mention it."

"Oops," said Willard.

"Oops, indeed, you big lug. For your information, Genevieve and I were discussing love and romance."

"That's right, Willard. And your dear wife said such a sweet thing. She said you were the romance of her life . . . her one and only."

"I'm beginning to regret that it may be too late to do anything about that," said Betsy-May.

"Darling, I'm so sorry. You're right, I am a big lug sometimes."

"It's all right if the man apologizes for himself . . . isn't it Genevieve?"

"Absolutely. No harm in that, dear. And, not to dwell on the subject, I had a lump removed nearly 25 years ago and haven't had a problem since."

"Ever had a lug removed?" asked Betsy-May.

"Ah, *touché*. Yes, as a matter of fact, several of them. But, let's forge ahead. Now, Willard . . . after your wife and I had ardently expressed ourselves for several minutes concerning the subject of love and romance, our birthday boy here made reference to the play reading this evening."

"I thought it was hysterical, Genevieve," said Willard. "Funniest thing I've heard for long as I can remember. Mac, don't tell me you was put off by it or something, 'cause listen to me . . . I love America . . . fought for it, almost died for it . . . do it again if I had to. Ain't no country in the world like . . ."

"Willard, please . . . don't get yourself all riled up at Mac. For what we know, he might have soldiered himself through that Vietnam thing."

"No he didn't."

"You don't know that."

"Yes I do."

"Mac?"

"I was in 'Nam."

"See, Willard. Wrong again."

"When was you in 'Nam, Mac?"

"1988, for a week. Stayed at the Continental Hotel in Saigon. Had a great time. Friendly people, good French restaurants, lovely tree-lined boulevards. Crawled through the Cu Chi tunnels, took a boat trip along the Mekong Delta. . . . Yeah, it was fun—and cheap, too. No fuss, no bother, had a real nice cyclo driver took me wherever I wanted to go, nobody shot at me . . ."

"All right, Mac, we get the point," Willard said. "Now, you get my point—ain't nothin' in this world can't do with a little bit of humor, see?"

"Even death?"

"Maybe especially death. You're Irish, right?"

"Of Irish descent, yes."

"So I assume, having managed to reach the age of fifty, you've attended a few Irish wakes in your time."

"Yes. I think I see where you're going."

"Where?"

"Everyone tends to have a pretty good time at an Irish wake. A lot of anecdotes, alcohol, and laughter. Had more fun at my father's wake than I did at my own wedding."

"Nobody has fun at their own wedding, for Christsakes, Mac. Most men I know had much more fun after their wives' funerals than they had at their weddings."

"Let's not forget the fun women have at their husbands' funerals, dear," said Betsy-May. "Oh, Genevieve, darling, I hope that doesn't offend you. Am I being insensitive to your feelings?"

"You most certainly are," Genevieve replied. "And I heartily approve of you for it. There is no one I find more tiresome than a farcical sentimentalist pretending to sympathize with my personal feelings of bereavement. Feeling sorry for other people for whatever reason is nothing more than a selfish, self-serving display of chicanery."

"Genevieve, it's a funny thing," said Willard. "I never in my life heard that last word you just used, but I know exactly what it means."

"What?"

"Fraud."

"Good for you, Willard. And I very much agree with what you had to say about the boundless applications of humor. You may, however, have been premature in your implied assumptions about Mac's feelings on the subject. Somehow the poor boy keeps being interrupted. So, pass your glasses everyone. Let's have a refill and then settle in to listen while Mac speaks his mind."

It took a minute or so for the grand dame to properly decant the effervescence, and while she was doing so, the two elderly Thai VIPs departed the room with their young consorts and posse of security personnel. Betsy-May drew our attention to the scene by saying, "Good riddance to bad rubbish." For better or worse, the volume she lent to that remark was sufficient to catch the attention of the porcine-faced ex-prime minister. Being in possession of just the right combination of alcohol and understanding of English, he stopped in his tracks, looked right, and proceeded to waddle his way directly towards our table. It couldn't have been more than a five-meter waddle, but he covered roughly twenty meters getting halfway to us. By that time, one of the bodyguards was at his side lending support. Sompong had noticed the developing situation and was immediately out from behind the bar. He very tactfully positioned himself in front of the human caricature of a swine, bowed graciously, and conferred quietly with the fellow. After a moment, he turned and approached our table.

"I'm very sorry to interrupt you, ladies and gentlemen, but it seems that one of our guests feels he has been insulted by someone at your table. I have explained to him that you are all most nice people."

"What do you mean 'almost nice people,' sir?" demanded Genevieve in a mock serious tone, and we all started laughing.

"Uh?" said Sompong.

The outburst of laughter had obviously served to further enrage the VIP, and he resumed his staggering, circuitous route in the direction of our table.

"Oh my Buddha!" exclaimed Sompong. "This is not good. This is really, really not good. You are causing that man to lose face."

"Now Sompong, dear, don't get your knickers all tied up in a knot," said Betsy-May. "Just relax. After all, causing a man who looks like that to lose face would be doing him a favor."

Howls of laughter erupted following that remark. Even Sompong was trying desperately not to crack up.

Another bodyguard had by now joined the approaching entourage and it was clear that the eyes of all those still remaining in the Bamboo Bar were fairly well focused on our table. Even the honeymooning Dutch couple had managed to disengage their simmering loins and stood like Siamese twins affixed at the hips on the top step to the upper alcove of the room. There was no doubt in my mind that those two could divorce and re-marry half a dozen times in the future and never enjoy themselves nearly as well as they were doing tonight. For all I know, they may already have been divorced and re-married half a dozen times. Considering the youthful age of the two lovebirds, that was highly unlikely. Nevertheless, the thought occurred to me. In retrospect, I am sure that was a subject of idle speculation, which I indulged simply as a means of distracting my attention from what seemed to be an imminent confrontation fraught with perilous consequences.

Genevieve leaned over to me and said, "Mac, would you please stand up and pull your chair away from the table. I think it's time to diffuse this situation before somebody else gets killed in here tonight. Now, all of you, no matter what happens, try not to laugh."

I did as she asked, and in less than five seconds she had wheeled herself around the table and came to an abrupt stop directly in front of the raging swine. It happened so quickly that the man didn't have time to stop himself. Despite being supported by the two bodyguards, he slammed his ankle into the vacant metal footrest of the wheelchair, screamed in pain, stumbled to his knees, and fell face forwards straight between the cleavage of Genevieve's aforementioned, ample bosom. (I have aforementioned that, right?)

Genevieve clasped her arms around the back of his head, hugging him so close that his screams of pain soon sounded as if he was in the throes of passion. The two bodyguards had, by this time, released their commandant and stood by looking totally dumbfounded by his predicament.

Genevieve turned briefly to us, winked devilishly, and said, "By the grace of Almighty God, would someone please remove this snout from my tender breasts." She thereupon grabbed him by the ears, brought him up to her face, and exclaimed, "What do you take me for, sir, some sort of floozy, pole-swinging, Patpong bargirl?"

"You tell him!" somebody yelled.

"Good for you, lady!" also made it onto the airwaves.

The bodyguards stepped in to retrieve their charge. He was obviously flabbergasted.

"Terribly sorry, madam. Terribly, terribly sorry. I certainly don't take you for . . . for . . . what did you say?"

"Some sort of floozy, pole-swinging, Patpong bargirl."

"Oh yes. No . . . I certainly don't take you for . . ."

"Oh you don't, do you? I suppose I'm not good enough for that, huh? Now you add insult to injury, sir. You certainly seemed to find some pleasure while trespassing upon my breasts."

"No!"

"No?"

"Well, I mean . . ."

"I'm very proud of my breasts, sir. And, I'll have you know, it's not just anybody that I allow to feast upon them."

"I shouldn't think so, madam."

"Yes, well, see that you don't. Most men who have had the pleasure were gracious enough to find some way to express their gratitude."

"I am most grateful. Really I am," he stammered.

One of the bodyguards made the sound of clearing his throat.

"Words, words, words," Genevieve chortled. "That's part of the lyric from a song in *My Fair Lady*. Are you familiar with it, sir?"

"The song?" he asked.

"The song, the musical, Lerner and Lowe . . . the sentiment, anything?"

"This bottle's a goner, Genevieve," said Willard.

Sompong whispered the obvious into the man's ear.

"Ah," said the barnyard boar. "Sompong, another bottle of Dom Perignon for these welcome guests of our country. Please . . ." and he reached into his pocket and handed Sompong a credit card. Then, addressing Genevieve, he said, "Please accept this gift, along with my apology. I certainly meant no disrespect."

"Very well, sir. Your apology is accepted. And my friends and I will be most grateful to enjoy your gift of champagne. Perhaps you'd care to join us."

"That's very kind of you madam, but it would seem that I've had more than enough to drink tonight already. My friends are waiting for me. I really must go. Please enjoy the rest of your evening."

Sompong returned, handing the man his credit card. He bowed, turned, and exited the bar.

Willard and Betsy-May broke into hysterics.

"Genevieve, you're one hell of a woman," Willard managed to say while catching his breath. "If that man had stuck around a moment longer, I don't think I could have kept a lid on my laughter. How in God's name did you plan such an outrageous sketch?"

"Planning had nothing to do with it, my dear fellow. It was sheer improvisation. You might say everything just sort of fell into place. Personally, I liked the final touch about inviting him to join us for a drink."

"Of course, you *knew* that he wouldn't," said Betsy-May.

"Of course."

"I loved the bit about the floozy, pole-swinging bargirl. Betsy-May and I were over in Patpong a couple nights ago, weren't we, sugar-plum? Some a' them doll-faced little vixens could kick-start a corpse."

"So I noticed," said Betsy-May.

"Ah, sugar, you know you're the only gal for me."

"Oh, I ain't complainin', mind you. We had the best lovin' tumble a couple hours later we'd had in a month of Sundays. Wish we had one a' them there bars back home."

Sompong, himself, arrived at our table bearing the fresh bottle of Dom Perignon, all snug in a silver bucket cascading with a glistening avalanche of crushed ice. One of the adorable-looking waitresses accompanied him carrying a bamboo tray filled with an assortment of steaming Thai *hors d'oeuvres*—spicy fried fishcakes, barbecued shrimp, crimsoned crab legs, chicken wings, a bowl of egg-fried rice, and . . . and some egg-shaped breaded items that I couldn't readily identify. An early-morning sky-blue porcelain vase of pink orchids, popcorn-like kernels of jasmine, and—the love of my life—sweet white and yellow blooms of frangipani contributed that unmistakable Thai charm to the whole provision set before us.

As Genevieve tendered her talents towards uncorking the Dom, and the waitress ever so charmingly arranged our table to accommodate the various *hors d'oeuvres*, Sompong assembled himself into an erect and rather venerable posture. Facing Genevieve, he said, "Madam, you are a remarkable woman. You may not believe this, but I enjoyed very much your play this evening. You have a very nice sense of humor, and I think humor is a better tonic than any I have seen behind a bar. It also just turned a very ugly situation into something very amusing. I salute you, madam."

"Well, that's very nice of you, Sompong. Thank you. And thank you for these delicious-looking treats."

"We make up some trays like this every evening, just in case somebody special comes in. No one has been in here tonight more special than you."

"Sompong, I sincerely hope you have a loving and deserving woman in your life. It would be a shame to spend all that charm on the few old bits and pieces of what are left of me."

"Genevieve," I said, "false modesty is clearly not one of your strengths. Nice try, though."

"Ha! You continue to surprise me, birthday boy. I like that in a man."

"Well then, madam," said Sompong, "let me surprise you also. I took the liberty of adding something extra to this collection of *hors d'oeuvres.*"

"These?" I said, pointing to the breaded egg-shaped items.

"Exactly," he replied. "Now please, all of you try one first. Then I'll tell you what they are."

Everyone sort of hesitated, but after Genevieve popped one into her mouth and declared it to be delicious, we all followed suit. I had two of them and, in fact, they were delicious—fetchingly spicy and just a tad on the gamy side.

"All right, Sompong," I said. "What the hell are they?"

"Pig's balls," he declared proudly. "Deep-fried pig's balls. They seemed an appropriate choice after what happened here ten minutes ago."

"And to the looks of the character it happened to, I might add," said Willard.

"Exactly, sir."

"Sompong, you're a genius. Could you join us for a glass of champagne?"

"There's nothing I would rather do, madam, but duty calls. I must return to the bar. Thank you for the offer. Now please, you all continue to enjoy yourselves. Anything you need, just let me know."

He bowed, turned, and walked back behind the bar.

"That's the second man in the last ten minutes who's turned me down for a glass of champagne. I must be losing my touch."

"Don't worry about it, Genevieve," I said. "I'm still here."

"Ah, so you are . . . so you are. Thank God for small favors, I always say."

"Ah, what a night . . . what a night," sighed Willard. "Fill 'em up, Genevieve. One more and, what you think, sugar? Time to hit the hay and whatnot, eh?"

"Hit the hay and whatnot? Whatnot sounds interesting, darlin'."

We all abandoned conversation for a while to rummage through the *hors d'oeuvres*. A second helping of pig's balls was supplied without our even asking. God, they were tasty!

Out of the corner of my eye—the left one, as I recall—I noticed the honeymooning Dutch couple approaching our table. They looked remarkably fresh and wrinkle-free considering . . . well, considering the manner in which they'd been engaging themselves for much of the evening.

"Sorry to intrude," said the young man addressing Genevieve, "but I am told you are the woman who wrote the play that was read here this evening. My new wife and I very much enjoyed it."

"Well, that's very kind of you. Thank you very much," Genevieve replied. "Your new wife, you say?"

"Yes, madam."

"Have you others of less recent vintage?"

"Ha! No, no. Marie-Jose is my first and I hope only wife. We were just married a couple of days ago and are here on our honeymoon. My name is Jahn."

"Well, my name is Genevieve and, Marie-Jose and Jahn, it's a pleasure to meet you. Congratulations on your marriage. I trust you've been enjoying yourselves."

I couldn't resist making a slight cough at that remark.

Jahn looked at me briefly with a rather impish grin on his face and said, "We've been enjoying ourselves quite nicely. Perhaps more so than is the usual custom in a place like the Bamboo Bar."

"The usual custom in places like the Bamboo Bar can become extremely tiresome after a while, my dear boy. Although, I must say, this evening seems to have been refreshingly out of the ordinary. I don't imagine people get shot to death here on a regular basis."

"Ah, the man in the brown suit," I said.

"That's right," said Genevieve. "A man who had any sense of fashion would never be caught dead wearing a brown suit after dark."

"However, in all fairness," I added, "I don't suppose he expected to be caught dead in it this evening."

"That's rather beside the point, I think," said Genevieve.

"Quite true."

"The little scene you had with the big-shot politician or whatever he is was also very amusing," said Jahn. "I assume that was not one of this evening's scheduled events."

"Oh no," said Genevieve. "That was entirely unrehearsed. A bit of improv-theater you might say."

"Marie-Jose and I were just at the top of the stairs on our way out when we saw that. Yes, all in all, a very enjoyable evening."

"How's about you and the little missus join us for a drink," offered Willard.

"Ah, thank you very much sir, but I think we've had plenty for this evening, and we're planning to visit the Floating Market early in the morning. Thanks again for the entertainment, and a pleasant good-night to you all."

I considered thanking them for their contribution to the evening's entertainment, but that would then require explanations that didn't seem appropriate to the situation. As they exited the scene, I noticed that the door was held open for them, which one might expect in a classy place like the Bamboo Bar. No one had opened the door for me, but I figured young, good-looking newlyweds rank privileges that balding, rank, fifty-year-old birthday bums don't. Then in walked Father Sean. He was the door-opening gentleman. When he reached the bar, Sompong nodded in our direction and I waved him over. After being introduced to everyone at the table, he accepted Genevieve's invitation to sit down. A waitress promptly delivered a Jameson.

"I was going to offer you a glass of champagne," said Genevieve, "but I see that this establishment is better acquainted with your tastes."

"Yes, they take very good care of me here, Genevieve. However, I must say that though I prefer the contents of my glass, the glass itself is no match for your own. Lalique crystal, if I'm not mistaken."

"Indeed it is," said Genevieve.

"Father Sean's slumming it in the Noel Coward Suite here," I said.

"The Noel Coward Suite, you say? My goodness!"

"Father Sean, is it?"

"Affirmative on both counts," I said.

"You're a Catholic priest?" asked Willard.

"That I am, sir. Although, as I thought I'd made plain to Mac, it's not a matter that needs be dwelt upon."

"Oops."

"Never mind, Mac. No need to stand on ceremony with me, folks. Please just call me Sean."

"Standing on ceremony, as you say, with Catholic priests, is not what you might be calling a temptation for me," said Willard. "Oh, and by the way, I mean that in the nicest way."

"Honestly, Willard!" exclaimed Betsy-May. "Now look who's being rude. You've only just met the man."

"It's not the man; it's the collar. But you're right, sugar. That was rude of me. I apologize. Had me more than my share of trouble with priests when I was a boy. Sorry."

"Quite all right, Willard," said Sean. "I had trouble with some of them when I was young, and I'm still having trouble with some of 'em. Bloody self-righteous hypocrites they can be. But I disagree with you on one point. It isn't the collar; it's the man wearin' it what makes the difference. Bishop took my collar away once. Now I got it back. But with or without it, my chosen mission is to serve God, and a big part of that mission is to treat others as I'd have them treat me. It's a shame, Willard, and I'm sorry that you suffered at the hands of fellow brethren of mine who strayed from that mission. Try not to hold it against all of us. And that's the end of that sermon. Amen."

"All right, amen," said Willard. "I'll drink to that. You knock back that whiskey and, sugar, hang on to your hat . . . I'm gonna do something I never thought I'd ever do. Gonna buy a drink for a Catholic priest."

"Well, glory be!" said Betsy-May. "If that ain't a miracle then Lazarus never rose from the dead. Now *that's* the man I married."

The five of us chatted amiably on and off while the singer and jazz musicians commenced what was to be their final set of the evening. Willard had accepted Sean's offer of an Esplendido, and between the two of them they puffed enough smoke into the room to remind me of a few North Halsted Street jazz clubs I used to h-ng out at in Chicago. . . . T

ere used to be a place called Lilly's just a block up from the B ograph Theater—the movie house where John Dillinger had a d te with a lady in red to see Clark Gable in a flick called *Manhattan M lodrama*. He walked left out of the theatre and got shot to death i an alley just around the corner. Fifty years later, if you walked r ght out of the theater, you could be listening to Blind John Davis a Lilly's. Take a date there, dressed in red or whatever color she l ked, and watch her marvel at the way Blind John fingered the b acks and whites. You just knew she was wishin' she could stretch o t in front of him, take advantage of his blindness, and hope for a moment or two he might mistake her for a piano.L

The publisher apologizes for the computer error on this page. Please find the correct text as follows:

The five of us chatted amiably on and off while the singer and jazz musicians commenced what was to be their final set of the evening. Willard had accepted Sean's offer of an Esplendido, and between the two of them they puffed enough smoke into the room to remind me of a few North Halsted Street jazz clubs I used to hang out at in Chicago. . . .

There used to be a place called Lilly's just a block up from the Biograph Theater—the movie house where John Dillinger had a date with a lady in red to see Clark Gable in a flick called *Manhattan Melodrama*. He walked left out of the theater and got shot to death in an alley just around the corner. Fifty years later, if you walked right out of the theater, you could be listening to Blind John Davis at Lilly's. Take a date there, dressed in red or whatever color she liked, and watch her marvel at the way Blind John fingered the blacks and whites. You just knew she was wishin' she could stretch out in front of him, take advantage of his blindness, and hope for a moment or two he might mistake her for a piano.

Lilly's was all white stucco and cushions and archways from room to room, and lazy ceiling fans and lots of smoke.

lly's was all white stucco and cushions and archways from room to room, and lazy ceiling fans and lots of smoke. There weren't any premium, name-brand liquors and wines. All the booze was what is known in the trade as 'rail stock.' But, it was cheap and plentiful and it got you through the night—like those sweet little dreams we leave on our pillows. Lilly's was a nice place to go on hot summer evenings when it seemed that even the walls were sweating and the jazzy Blind John Davis was the coolest thing in town.

Round about half past midnight, Sompong soft-shoed his way over to our table and notified Willard that the 1:00 a.m. ferry across the river to the Peninsula Hotel would be leaving in thirty minutes. It was based upon this information, by the way, that I figured it was round about half past midnight at the time. Not that I mean to brag, of course, but I've always been good with numbers.

Apparently the ferry service ends at 1:00 a.m.

The Peninsula Hotel is the newest five-star establishment on the river, and no expense was spared in its construction. It has quickly attained a reputation as being one of the finest hotels in the world. Naturally, we were all duly impressed that a couple of Appalachian hickseeds like Willard and Betsy-May had managed to get themselves ensconced there. (That's just a bit of gratuitous facetiousness, folks.) As it turned out, Willard and Betsy-May were pretty damn impressed as well. They virtually rhapsodized in describing their room: twentieth-floor view of the river; firm, spacious bed with lots of soft, cozy pillows filled with what Willard likened to duck feathers.

"Used to shoot me some ducks, ya know," he said. "And the carpet is so plush it's like walking barefoot on the Bermuda grass fairways of a . . . a . . ."

"A US Open golf course," Sean suggested.

"Exactly. You play golf, Father?" asked Willard. And it was curious the way he casually and yet purposely addressed Sean respectfully as "Father." Betsy-May combed her fingers through his hair. What a dear, sweet couple they made.

"Don't get me started on the game of golf, Willard, if you're plannin' to catch that last ferry across the river. Hate to see you and Betsy-May havin' to swim home tonight."

"Well, okay then," said Willard, "maybe some other time. Great game, though."

"That it is."

"Closest Willard's got to swimmin' since we been here is in the sunken marble bathtub in our room," said Betsy-May. "Gracious me is it fancy. Color television built right into the wall, and two telephones—one on the wall beside the bathtub and another one next to the toilet."

"I could spend near the rest of my life in that there tub," said Willard. "Yesterday afternoon when Betsy-May was out doin' a bit of shoppin', I sat in that tub full of warm water, Epsom salts, couple ounces of olive oil . . . ordered me up a bacon-cheeseburger with french fries and a nice cold beer and watched a golf tournament. Yes sir, that bathtub has to be the coziest place I been since my mama's womb. Probably more so when you throw in the TV and the telephone. What do you reckon, sugar-plum?"

"Well, never havin' been in your mama's womb, darlin', I can't really say, but it's not just the bathroom I fancy. There's the teakwood paneled bar, private fax machine, light dimmers, remote controlled window curtains, wonderful surround-sound music system, and large dressing room with lots of closet space."

"Oh, and don't forget that little cubbyhole," said Willard. "You put your shoes inside there, and twenty minutes later, like magic, they're all polished up brand new. Betsy-May and me . . . we been so well taken care of since we landed in Bangkok, I swear, it's like we died and gone to heaven."

"Well listen, love of my life," said Betsy-May, "let's say we get back to the room 'fore we die."

"You up for a bit a' heaven tonight, sugar-plum?"

"Bein' up is your part of the bargain, darlin'. But I'm game if you are."

Willard walked over to the bar, settled his tab, and brought Sompong back to the table with him. Everyone was hugging and kissing good-bye, and Willard said, "Damn, it's like we're all from California around here!"

After the two elderly lovebirds had gone to roost back at the Peninsula, I proceeded to acquaint Genevieve and Sean with the salient bits of information about themselves that I had become familiar with earlier in the evening.

Genevieve was particularly fascinated with Sean's odyssey during his involuntary leave of absence from the altar of his little parish on the Emerald Isle:

"Bloody bastard," she said, referring to the bishop who had sent Sean packing. "I started playing chess when I was a young girl and I haven't trusted bishops ever since. They're devious. Zig-zagging assassins . . . that's what bishops are."

Eventually the subject of the play reading re-surfaced, and I again indicated that considering how Genevieve and Betsy-May had been waxing sentimental about love and romance, it seemed to me that the play itself dealt rather cynically with those two themes.

Genevieve responded by saying, "First of all, it may surprise you to know that the idea for the play occurred to me more than 25 years ago."

"You're quite right, Genevieve," I said. "I am surprised. . . . Sean, would you care to make it unanimous?"

"All right," he said. "I'm surprised as well."

At the Bamboo Bar

"Somehow I like the way he said it better than the way you did, Mac. Must be the Irish accent. It's enough to make your knees buckle. Of course, only one of them in my case, but be that as it may. Anyway, do either of you remember a movie that came out in 1974 or '75 called *The Towering Inferno*?"

The Towering Inferno was, perhaps, the first in the cinematic genre of great American disaster films. Crashing jumbo jets, sinking cruise ships and, in this case, a tall building catching on fire. In every case there's lots of screaming and yelling and panic and drama and sappy romances and heroes and villains, and many people die but, thank God, there's always a cute little dog or some retarded, epileptic child with a clubfoot who survives and . . . oh, for Christsakes, if you've seen one you've seen them all, and you know what I'm talking about. One of the distinguishing features of these films is that they often comprise a cast of top-name Hollywood stars in cameo roles. This makes it possible for directors to kill off actors and actresses for whom the general audience already has an inbred sympathy. It makes their death scenes much more poignant. In *The Towering Inferno*, for example, I, personally, was very distressed when Fred Astaire, of all people, lost his footing and slipped out a window from the 932nd floor.

Anyway, it was the tragic story of an extremely tall building catching fire, as depicted in this movie, which first inspired Genevieve to begin composing the sketch that was read this evening at the Bamboo Bar. Presumably there are other somewhat similar events that occurred in the succeeding years, which have a certain relationship to her *Rock Bottom Good-bye* farce. One in particular was alluded to before we left the bar—alluded to without actually being mentioned. Nevertheless, I'm sure it was on all of our minds, and it had the effect of briefly checking the conversation. In retrospect, it was clearly this awkward lull that prompted Genevieve's next move. She reached into the cleavage of her dress and plucked out a thin, two-inch square, plastic Ziploc pouch.

"I make it a habit to carry this wherever I go," she explained. "Inside are two small pieces of paper upon which I have inscribed what are, undoubtedly, two of my favorite quotes of all time. The plastic casing, though lacking the appropriate elegance of style, preserves them against . . . moisture. Moisture either of my own making or that of the slobbering male admirers I still manage to attract from time to time."

The most recent instance of Genevieve's body being prey to a slobbering male admirer had been one of the salient bits of information about her that I had previously brought to Sean's attention.

"Maybe you should get yourself a rape whistle," I suggested.

"I bought one of those years ago," she said. "They're useless. Blew the damn thing till I was blue in the face . . . nobody ever raped me. I finally threw it away."

Sompong suddenly materialized upon the scene like a genie from a vase. "I beg your pardon," he began, "but . . ."

"Never beg, my dear man," said Genevieve. "Begging is for beggars. And, although some of them probably make more money than the both of us, it is, nevertheless, an occupation that resides well below your esteemed self. So, no more of this begging nonsense, sir. Simply state your case. We're all ears."

"Indeed we are," said Sean

"Like a cornfield in Kansas," I added

"Well," continued Sompong, "it is my sad duty to inform you that the bar will be closing in less than an hour.

"Oh dear. All good things must come to an end, I suppose."

"Yes, Mac, but there's no need to be hasty about it," added Genevieve. She was thereupon distracted by the entrance of a young couple whom I recognized as the Muffy and Brad characters from the play reading. Genevieve flagged them over. Sean and I stood up and they were introduced as Jeanette Schwaba and James Osborne. Both appeared to be in their early thirties. Jeanette had blond hair, green eyes, and a very nicely contoured pair of legs that were revealed through the front cut of her turquoise, midcalf-length skirt. James had brown hair, blue eyes, and was wearing a pair of loose-fitting, triple pleated, gray trousers, which I'm sorry to say made it impossible for me to assess the shapeliness of his legs. I think it goes without saying that both these young people were attired in various other bits and pieces of apparel besides a skirt and a pair of trousers, so . . . I'm not going to say.

Genevieve ordered another bottle of Dom.

Sompong nodded towards the champagne flutes used by Willard and Betsy-May saying, "Shall I freshen those up for the next round, madam?"

"Yes, please," replied Genevieve. "They're promiscuous little nymphs, aren't they?" As Sompong walked away, Jeanette added, "I suppose it's only fair that he refers to you as 'madam.'"

"Ha!" said James. "You walked right into that one, *madam*."

"Ah, young people today," sighed Genevieve. "No respect for their elders."

She then went on to explain that Jeanette and James had both studied at the comedy-improv workshops of the famed Second City Theater in Chicago. They eventually became members of its touring company, and it was while Genevieve was visiting her younger brother, a professor of chemistry at the University of Chicago, that she had the opportunity of seeing them perform.

Genevieve had been living in New York for thirty some odd years, engaged in some odd pursuits and basically enjoying the good life courtesy of a few odd million dollars inherited from her husband who had worked himself to death as owner-operator of two of the most exclusive funeral homes in the city. She claims to have started writing plays while attending Smith College in Washington, D.C., and turned to comedy sketches after receiving a Rhodes scholarship to Oxford. Allegedly, several of her works were produced in London and off Broadway in New York. Otherwise, she was a dutiful wife who traveled extensively around the world with her husband. She had met the current general manager of the Oriental at a cocktail party held several years ago at the Hotel Crillion bar in Paris. They apparently took a liking to each other and he offered her an open invitation to hold a play reading at the Bamboo Bar if she ever visited Bangkok.

As for the missing limb, "I'd like to say that it happened while scaling Mount Everest, or in a shark attack off the Great Barrier Reef," she said, "but, in truth, it fell prey to a rare degenerative condition which finally necessitated its removal about five years ago. Still, I got a lot of mileage out of it and, God willing, I've plenty more miles to go. In the meantime, I'm becoming very comfortable in this chair. And, I find people to be kinder than they used to be, which makes me feel kinder, so that's a plus."

"Perhaps the world would be a better place if we were all in wheelchairs," James suggested facetiously.

"I like these two better when they're on stage," said Genevieve, referring to Jeanette and James. "Up close and personal, they can get on your nerves after a while."

"Ah, you love us, Genevieve," said Jeanette.

Sompong reappeared with a fresh bottle of Dom cradled in a silver ice bucket, and the two Lalique champagne flutes.

While refilling the glasses, Genevieve informed us that Jeanette's father is a highly respected medical research scientist at Northwestern University in Chicago.

"You don't say so?" said Sean.

"I most emphatically do say so," Genevieve retorted. "Am I right or am I right, Jeanette?"

"You're right, Genevieve, as always," said Jeanette. "My father was one of the early pioneers in the field of animal cloning."

"Oh, how fascinating. Pigs and sheep and rabbits and whatnot?"

"Yes, exactly."

"How early a pioneer in this field was he?" I asked.

"He's been at it for nearly 35 years now, Mac."

"Ah."

"'Ah' what, Mac?" said Genevieve.

"Well, I was just wondering if you hadn't had a recent encounter with one of his inaugural test cases."

That remark elicited "ha has" from Genevieve and Sean, and "uhs?" from James and Jeanette.

Addressing the befuddled thespians, Genevieve explained:

"Mac is referring to an incident which occurred this evening just prior to your entering the arena. I found myself engaged in a sort of burlesque comedy of manners with a mid-sixtyish Thai gentleman of dubious distinction whose overall appearance, particularly in the neighborhood of his face, suggested that he may have been of a mixed heritage that wasn't, shall we say, exclusively human."

"You mean his visage seemed to indicate a hybrid of species?" asked James. "What was he, for God's sake, a politician?"

"Yes, but even more of an amalgamation than that. His ears were pinkish and rather fleshy—floppy sort of appendages . . . and, where a nose should have been was a bulbous snout. And, where that bulbous snout should not have been was snorting itself between my bosom as if it were on the scent of some rare truffles."

"Oh, Genevieve! What a traumatic experience," declared Jeanette. "Or, were you more likely, in the throes of ecstasy?"

"Naughty girl. Naughty, naughty, naughty."

"Now be honest," Jeanette teased.

"Well, all right, I confess that it wasn't an entirely unpleasant experience. God knows, as far as foreplay goes, I've certainly had worse."

And that remark elicited a tableful of "ha has."

"Oh, and to answer your question, Mac," said Jeanette, "it's a pretty safe bet that my father had nothing to do with altering the specimen with whom Genevieve apparently developed an attachment while James and I were out foraging for a meal."

"Foraging for a meal," cried Genevieve. "Oh you poor dears. You might just as well have stayed here and had Sompong bring you something from . . . from . . . well, from somewhere."

"No, we wanted to get out for a while. And, of course, there's no telling how people are going to react to this funny little sketch of yours, Genevieve."

"We found a noodle stand a few blocks away. Fried noodles and pork washed down with a small bottle of Mekhong whiskey. It was delicious."

"Pork of a genuine pig, I trust," said Sean.

"I certainly think so," said Jeanette. "Not likely that my father had anything to do with it. Although, in Thailand, they do refer to pork as *moo,* so I suppose one can't be entirely sure of its breeding."

"No doubt it's only a matter of time before this cloning business begins to apply itself to human beings," said James.

"Oh, absolutely," said Jeanette. "The opportunities for development are mind-boggling. And, of course, it's still a relatively new field of research."

"Virgin, you might say," added Genevieve.

"Well, exactly," said Sean. "And by its definition, guaranteed to remain so, regardless of how many years it persists. Perhaps I'm old-fashioned, but I fear it's a dicey business fooling around with Mother Nature."

"Yes, that's certainly a legitimate concern," Genevieve agreed. "But, you never know, some good might come from it. I mean, wouldn't it be a better world if they could clone Frenchmen with cheery dispositions, or Germans with a sense of humor?"

"How about if they could clone American and English politicians to mind their own business?"

"Yes! And Muslims to be less insecure of themselves and more tolerant of others."

"May the saints preserve us!" Sean sang out. "If they could manage all that, plus give the Chinese blue eyes and make the Jews drink more, we'd have a world full of Irishmen, wouldn't we?"

"Well . . . yes," someone stammered. "As you said, Sean, fooling around with Mother Nature is a dicey business."

"However, speaking of Irishmen," said Genevieve, "that reminds me. . . . Reverently encased within this rather common-looking bit of plastic are two slips of paper. Upon each is written a quote, and both of them are dear to my heart. . . . Mac, would you please be so kind as to have a look at this one and then read it aloud to us. It was written by Mr. Oscar Wilde in his story called *The Picture of Dorian Gray*."

As she held out the slip of paper, I said, "Wait a minute. Let me dry my hands first. You make me feel as if I'm about to wrap my paws around the ancient parchment of the Dead Sea Scrolls."

"I would be most obliged if you didn't wrap your paws around it," she implored. "You should manage to hold it between two fingers, thank you very much."

As it turned out, she was correct about that.

I perused the short quote gently clasped between thumb and index finger of my left hand. Then, looking up at her, I said, "Brilliant. Quite right I think, as well. One of Oscar's juiciest and most astute plums if you want my opinion. It reminds me of the day when, as a young boy of seven or eight, my mother took me and two of my fellow siblings to lunch in the Oak Room Bar at the Plaza Hotel in New York City. Our family was living in Northern New Jersey at that time. Father had been hired away from his job in Chicago by a large pharmaceutical company and, as was the custom in those days, we went with him."

"Mac," interrupted Genevieve. "I know it's your fiftieth birthday and all, but . . ."

"Oh now please, Genevieve," I interrupted back. "This is a nice memory of mine."

"Happy birthday," said Jeanette.

"Right on," said James. "Happy birthday, Mac. Cheers."

"Thanks. Cheers," I said. "So anyway, I remember having a chicken club sandwich on toast with french fries and a chocolate milkshake. It was all delicious. Best chicken sandwich I've ever had in my life. To tell you the truth, I forget what everybody else was having."

"What a pity," said Genevieve.

"Oh, give the man a break, dear," pleaded Jeanette. "It's his fiftieth birthday for Heaven's sake."

"Carry on, my lad," said Sean. "I take it there's some connection between that memorable luncheon and the Oscar Wilde quote?"

"Yes."

"And you're on the very threshold—most probably within a moment, if not less—of acquainting us with exactly what that connection is. Am I right?"

"Uh, sure. Absolutely . . . on the threshold . . . within a moment. Right."

"Well then, by all means please proceed."

"I'm not boring you?" I asked.

"Oh, it's too late to trouble yourself with a petty concern such as that," said Genevieve."

"I suppose that horse is out of the barn by now, huh?"

"Well into the next county I should think," she said. "Is there a finish line in sight?"

"Oh hell, sorry," I said. "Champagne and all making me nostalgic, I guess. But, here's the point. While we children were having apple pie à la mode, my mother told us the story of *The Picture of Dorian Gray*. She sat there with her tea and cucumber sandwiches and told us the whole story. She didn't read it to us, mind you. She told us in her own words as she remembered it. Probably took over an hour, but she was a great storyteller. She had us children totally enraptured. I remember it as if it were . . . well, not exactly yesterday but let's say, no more than a week ago last Tuesday."

"A week ago last Tuesday, you say. My goodness."

"Genevieve," Jeanette scolded.

"Okay, okay. Just let me say one more thing about this. Okay?"

"Of course, Mac," said Jeanette.

"Well, about a year later, I watched the movie of *The Picture of Dorian Gray* on TV. It was marvelous, but still, the way my mother had told the story was even better. Anyway, years after that, my mother showed me a short article in the *New York Times*. It referred to the death of George Sanders who, as you may know, was the British actor who played the part of Sir Henry in the movie version."

"I knew the man," said Genevieve. "Not intimately, but well enough not to be terribly surprised by the nature of his demise."

"And it's the character of Sir Henry," I continued, "that Wilde had speak the words of this quote you handed me."

"Right you are," said Genevieve. "A quote which I trust that sometime in the near future you are also going to speak. But, do carry on. Consider me as having become part of the crop in that cornfield in Kansas alluded to ages ago. I hereby resolve never to underestimate you again. You are a man of sneaky intelligence."

"Okay, I'll take that as a compliment, darling. In any case, the article indicated that Sanders had committed suicide somewhere in Spain, as I recall. What really got to me was the note he left behind—the suicide note. It was a very short note and the gist of it was, 'I'm bored.' He was bored with his life . . . he'd had enough of it. And so he killed himself.

"Even then, as a young man, I knew what boredom was, and that note has haunted me ever since. My mother obviously sensed something alarming in my reaction, and for a moment I think she regretted having shown me the story. Then she said to me, 'Sweetheart, boredom is all in the mind. Like beauty, it's in the eye of the beholder. Listen to your heart, for in your heart there are dreams, and someday one of them will seize the focus of your mind. Then all you have to do is pursue that dream wherever it leads you. It will involve struggle, but it's the struggle that makes the pursuit worthwhile. Boredom is what sets into our lives when we are no longer struggling in pursuit of a dream.'"

"Very good advice," said Sean. "Your mother is a very wise woman."

"Yes, she's had her moments. . . . Now, to the quote. I only hope that my discursive preamble has not induced amongst you all a state of mind similar to the one which lead to Mr. Sanders' premature exit from the stage."

I held up the slip of paper in the best area of light available and read it aloud as follows: "Humanity takes itself too seriously. It is the world's original sin. If the caveman had known how to laugh, History would have been different."

"Ah, well done my lad," said Sean. "You have an excellent speaking voice."

"Yes. Well done, indeed," echoed Genevieve. "I will even go so far as to say that it was worth the wait. I trust Oscar is grinning in his grave."

"Well," I said, "if a man who's proud of his Irish heritage can't read Wilde with a certain amount of panache, then what good is he?"

"And if an American, regardless of what his heritage may be," James stepped in, "cannot appreciate the humor of Genevieve's sketch, which was read here this evening, then I say the same thing—what good is he? Would you believe we actually got booed off the stage in Boston and New York?"

"Oh, put a sock in it, James," said Genevieve. "We knew what we were trying to do and they didn't. Leave them to their grief, if that's what they want. Most of them are only doing it from a sense of civic duty. They'll soon tire of wallowing in it. 'Humor equals pain plus time,' said Lenny Bruce. Give them some more time. Americans are very resilient. They have an unconquerable buoyancy of spirit. And speaking of spirit, let's put the remainder of this champagne to rest. And Sean, one more Irish whiskey for you, if you please?"

Genevieve then motioned to Sompong, whom it would seem had dedicated one of his orbs exclusively to our table. He was on the scene just as Genevieve had finished her expert transfusion of champagne to the crystal nymph quartet.

"Sompong, my dear man," she said while extending a hand beneath her chair. "Father Sean would be ever so grateful for a *bon voyage* Jameson whiskey. And as it is that he has an upcoming task to perform, make it a double shot. Put it on my bill and . . ." handing Sompong one of her Lalique brandy snifters, "please cozy it lovingly within this . . . this chalice."

Sompong gingerly cupped the snifter in his hand and replied, "Madam, your wish is my command."

He was back in a flash with the elegantly enshrined beverage, which he placed upon a new Bamboo Bar coaster in front of Sean. Then, turning towards Genevieve he said, "What, if you don't mind me asking, is Father Sean's task for which he will require this double shot of Irish whiskey to perform?"

"Our resident gentleman of the cloth is going to lend his mellifluous vocal chords to the recital of a quote by the great American humorist, Mark Twain."

"Ah, Mark Twain," said Sompong. "I had a friend in New York who worked at a bar called Huck Finn's. Very famous man, Mark Twain. I remember a quote of his."

"Do you now?" Sean asked.

"Oh yes," said Sompong. "They had many of his quotes on the walls around Huck Finn's. At the moment, however, I can only remember one of them."

"Well, I'll tell you what, my good fellow," said Sean. "You recite the quote for us right now that you remember, and if it's the same one written upon the slip of paper hitherto lodged within madam's bosom, I will gladly give you a nice, new, crisp 100-dollar bill."

"Why do I get the impression that I'm losing control of this whole quote-reading project," sighed Genevieve. "On a brighter note, however, I must say that it's been many years since my bosom was so closely related in the same sentence to a 100-dollar bill—crisp or otherwise, for that matter."

"Well, keep in mind," Jeanette pointed out, "that we're dealing with Irishmen here. They revel in their digressions. They are . . . how does it go. . . ? 'Too poetical to be poets . . .'"

"'A nation of magnificent failures . . .'"

"'But they're the greatest talkers since the Greeks.'"

"Ah, another Wilde quote if I'm not mistaken," said James.

"No," Genevieve said, "you are not mistaken. Although one of his more self-serving *bon mots*, I might add."

"I don't see what's so self-serving about referring to his motherland as a nation of failures—magnificent or not," suggested Jeanette.

"It's the other two bits that I think Genevieve was referring to," said James.

"And yet still," added Sean, "I'd much rather be a magnificent failure than a mediocre success. How boring would that be!"

"Far too boring a fate to contemplate on my fiftieth birthday, sir. That's for damn sure!"

"See, Genevieve," said Jeanette. "I rest my case. We're in the midst of an Irish brotherhood."

"I don't suppose you've noticed any Greeks in here this evening, Sompong?" asked Genevieve.

"Not as I recall, madam."

"Well that's a relief. Imagine the difficulty of normal people like you and I, Jeanette, trying to accomplish anything conversationally in a roomful of Greeks and Irishmen. Anyway, Sompong, I see the good Father has placed a 100-dollar bill on the table, so let's hear the Mark Twain quote you remember. The floor is yours. Cornfield in Kansas everyone."

"Okay, it goes like this: 'In India they worship every form of life except human life.' That's it; not very long. Probably why I remember it and why I have no desire to visit India."

"That quote was on the wall of Huck Finn's bar, was it?"

"Yes, madam. Amongst others, of course."

"Of course."

"Well, my good man," said Sean after having picked up Genevieve's slip of paper and given it a quick perusal, "I'm afraid this 100-dollar bill is destined to remain in my custody a while longer."

"Honestly!" declared Genevieve, in a tone of mock exasperation. "And people criticize the English for having exploited native populations. Imagine if the Irish had had any success with imperialism? Aren't you glad Thailand was never colonized, Sompong?"

"For the most part, I would say yes. Then again, knowing the nature of Thais as I do, had we been colonized I am certain that the colonizers would have ended up being far more exploited than us. As for Father Sean, he merely offered me a risk-free opportunity to gain 100 dollars. I should be very happy for more opportunities of that sort. Now I need to tend the bar for a moment or two but, if you don't mind, I would very much like to hear Father Sean read your Mark Twain quote, madam."

"We shall gladly await your return, Sompong," said Genevieve. "Take your time."

After turning and floating away as if upon a cloud, Sean said of him, "Such a splendid gentleman. If one were to think of the entire world as a bar, I'd like to have him tending it. But, keeping in mind Shakespeare's world-as-a-stage metaphor, let me have a good look at this Twain twaddle so that I shall be worthy of performing my role when Sompong returns."

"Twain twaddle, is it?" Genevieve barked. "Ha! It's a gem. I only hope that when Sompong does return, and you've had a little nip of the adult beverage, you'll then manage to proceed directly to the task at hand without a warping series of discursive childhood memoirs."

"Oh now, I enjoyed Mac's . . . Mac's . . . his, you know . . ."

"Warping series of discursive childhood memoirs," I said.

"Yes, those," continued Jeanette. "And they weren't at all warping, whatever that means. I think they were a charming embellishment. I'm sorry, Genevieve, but I guess this Irish blarney is contagious."

"In retrospect," Genevieve conceded, "I suppose we would all agree. Amazing how bewitching the Irish blarney can be. But time is of the essence now. The bar will be closing soon. So, if it isn't too much trouble . . ."

"No trouble, at all," said Sean looking up from the slip of paper. "It's a wonderful quote."

"Not twaddle?"

"Not at all, Genevieve. I should be happy to read it aloud. . . . Ah, Sompong, you're back. Now, one sip of whiskey to whet my whistle, as you Yanks say. . . . Oh, that's good. . . . And, here we go. I give you the words of the justly esteemed Mr. Mark Twain: 'The human race in its poverty, has unquestionably one really effective weapon—laughter. Power, money, persuasion. Supplication, persecution—these can lift at a colossal humbug—push it a little, weaken it a little, century by century; but only laughter can blow it to rags and atoms at a blast. Against the assault of laughter nothing can stand.'"

An appropriate moment of silence followed. Then everyone hastened to congratulate Sean on his excellent reading of the quote. He said something to the effect that he intended to find a way of incorporating it into the sermon at Sunday morning's Mass, and James said something to the effect that Americans ought to incorporate it into their daily prayers regardless of what religion, if any, that they subscribed to. Genevieve suggested that it wouldn't do James any harm to work on taking the message to heart for himself and stop worrying so much about other people's reactions to his performances of her work.

"I haven't the slightest inclination to either explain or try to justify my work," she declared. "People either understand the point of it or they don't. They can agree or disagree; like it or not like it. Naturally, I would prefer that people like it, but I'm not going to argue with them. It has never been my intention to purposely insult people. You essentially demean yourself whenever you attempt to demean others. Poking a bit of fun at people—that's something else. Satire is something else as far as I'm concerned. Nevertheless, there is nothing you can do or say in this world that is going to please everyone, and perhaps that's the way it should be—at least with regard to anything that's really worth doing or saying."

"But obviously these two quotes . . ." began Sean. "Well, what I mean to say is that it's not merely a coincidence that you keep them close to your heart."

"Nestled within the warmth of my bosom?"

"Exactly."

"You mean rather than wedged inside my shoe, for instance?"

"Yes, for instance."

"Well, you see," she reasoned, "I lost a foot once, and I've lost my heart several times. Each time, however, I eventually got my heart back. Never did get that foot back. I just figure my heart's a safer place to store things."

Nobody seemed inclined to take issue with that explanation, and, as it turned out, there wouldn't have been much time to do so anyway. The lights brightened, the bar bills were paid up and, while the other patrons ambled off, all members of our party took the time to especially thank Sompong for his gracious service. He collected the various Lalique glasses that had been in use and told us to just relax for the few minutes it would take to clean them.

During this respite, Genevieve happened to mention that she was working up a new sketch, which she had been invited to debut at the Globe Restaurant in Phnom Penh the following month. Sean offered that since he'd missed most of this evening's performance, maybe we'd all like to have a nightcap in the Noel Coward Suite and listen to a reading of the new sketch, such as it was. Jeanette and James liked the idea, and Genevieve suggested that perhaps the Noel Coward Suite might be just the place to lend a bit of inspiration to this work-in-process of hers. When the ensemble turned their eyes to me to pass the proposal unanimously, I said,

"Hell, yes! I was born in Chicago and it's still my birthday there. Fact is, I got about nine more hours to party."

The rest of them hastened to let me know that if I intended to carry on celebrating my birthday according to Chicago time, I'd be doing so minus their company. It was agreed that one more hour was as long as any of them would be willing to extend the festivities. Sean had been invited to say Sunday morning Mass at Assumption Church across the road. Genevieve needed her "beauty sleep." Jeanette was scheduled for a two-hour massage at the Oriental Health Spa, and James said he didn't really have an excuse, but if one came to him, he would let me know later.

When the Lalique crystal was returned clean and sparkling, we made our exit from the bar—James chauffeuring Genevieve. Two male members of the hotel staff who obviously knew their way around a weight room were waiting for us at the foot of the stairs leading up to the Author's Suites. They picked up Genevieve in her chair with about as much ease as, a moment later, I picked up the wooden matchstick propped against the bottom of the door to the suite.

I prepared the drinks while Sean led the party on a group tour of the place. Everyone was duly impressed, although Genevieve felt that the bedroom lacked an appropriate degree of coziness. She had the sense of it being something of a period piece you might find set up in a museum with a red velvet rope around it. Sean thereupon handed her a blue silk cushion, which she threw on the floor. That gave the room more of a "lived-in" feeling as far as she was concerned. When Sean pointed out that there was an extra bed available and suggested that the best way of lending a place the kind of lived-in ambience she was referring to, was to actually *live in* it, Genevieve paused for a moment to consider the proposition. . . .

"Well," she said, "that might be interesting. I've never slept with a priest before."

"And a gay priest at that," said Sean. "Now there's the sort of field research that could be developed into a very amusing sketch, I should imagine."

"Don't let your imagination get too far ahead of you, my dear padre. For the time being, shall we return to the front room? I'll give you a brief set-up on this work-in-process and then we can sit back and see what my two traveling troubadours can do with it."

Everyone settled down with a glass of port. Sean and I re-fired our cigars. The windows were open, the air cool and balmy.

Genevieve turned towards Jeanette and said, "When I was your age, it was unheard of for a woman to be in the presence of men once they had decanted the port and lit the cigars."

"My, haven't we come a long way since then, eh baby?" Jeanette replied. "I suppose any second now, these gentlemen are going to start discussing politics and solving the world's problems."

"The hell with politics," said James. "It bores the hell out of me."

"Are you still voting for those Libertarians?" asked Genevieve.

"Naturally."

"But they always lose," Jeanette pointed out.

"No," he said. "We lose when the other guys win."

"What are the Libertarians about?" asked Sean.

"They're about, basically, three things," said James. "Defend the territorial integrity of the United States, build interstate roads, and take care of those people who genuinely—and I repeat, *genuinely*—are unable to take care of themselves. Otherwise, get the hell out of the way and let people alone."

"America's the most powerful nation in the world," said Sean. "They've made mistakes, but I think it would be a very big mistake to adopt an isolationist policy with regard to the rest of the world."

"Well, here we go, Genevieve," said Jeanette. "The boys are going to start solving the world's problems. Please say something to bail us out before this turns into an all night yak-fest."

"All right, I'll say one thing. There's much talk about the United States being the world's policeman. Fine. Just make an amendment to the Constitution which stipulates that all candidates for President of the country must have at least one child old enough to qualify for military service. Boy or girl; it doesn't matter. Then, whenever it's determined that the US should involve itself militarily in response to a world crisis, that child suits up and reports to the front line of combat. Very simple—lead by example. In fact, every member of the United Nations ought to follow the same rule."

No one seemed readily inclined to try and top that, so we all made ourselves comfortable in anticipation of the performance.

Genevieve passed a copy of the script to Jeanette and James. She introduced it as follows:

"The sketch, at least for the time being, is set in the rather swank office of Miss Pamela Worthington. She is the sales director of Christie's auction house in London. An American gentleman by the name of Charles Franklin is in the office with her. The purpose of the meeting is to go through the formalities of payment with regard to an item at the auction for which he had made the winning bid.

"We're still 'on book' with this one, as they say in the theater, so James and Jeanette will be reading from the script and I shall handle the references to the character Agnes. Try not to let that be a distraction. . . . Now, you two are looking very comfortable on the sofa next to the photo of Mr. Noel Coward. The house is packed to the rafters and the curtain has just gone up. . . ."

"Mr. Franklin, I'd like to begin by congratulating you on your winning bid at this afternoon's auction."

"Thank you. Thank you very much."

"You are now the proud owner of the famous yellow and green number 10 jersey worn by the incomparable Pele during the final of the 1970 World Cup."

"Yes. So I am."

"I might also add that your bid of 157,750 pounds is far and away the highest price ever paid for a used football jersey that we here at Christie's have hitherto had the privilege of getting rid . . . I mean, of passing off . . . passing *on*, rather, to our esteemed clientele. I hope I made myself clear there."

"Yes, quite clear. Thank you. It happens, however, to be the highest price ever paid at *any* auction house for a 'used'—as you so charmingly put it—soccer jersey."

"Ah yes, soccer. You're American, Mr. Franklin, of course. In America people refer to football as soccer, don't they?"

"No, in America we refer to *football* as football. And, we refer to soccer as *soccer*."

"Yes, well, when in Rome and all that. Far be it from the English to stand on a technicality of that nature with an American. God knows we learned our lesson about that sort of thing 250 years ago, what? Ha, ha . . ."

"One might have thought so, yes."

"Right. May I offer you a drink, Mr. Franklin? Something stiff, perhaps. Scotch, bourbon, a small bottle of gin. . . ?"

"Sorry, is it Mrs., Miss, or Ms. Worthington? Your card didn't seem to indicate one way or the other."

"No it doesn't. I like to retain a certain degree of mystery. It's the female prerogative, don't you know."

"Ah, yes. In any case, I just meant to apologize if I seem a tad surly. My mind has been elsewhere. Something stiff is probably exactly what I need, to loosen up. If it isn't too much trouble, a Scotch and soda might be just what the doctor ordered."

"No trouble at all, Mr. Franklin.

(She presses the button on her desktop intercom and a female voice responds: "Yes, Miss Worthington?")

"Agnes, dear, we'd like a couple of adult beverages in here, please. A Scotch and soda, easy on the soda, and the usual for me, thank you."

"Well, *Miss* Worthington, so much for *that* degree of mystery. I suppose you're going to leave me guessing for as long as possible as to what your *usual* adult beverage is."

"The *usual* is a very dry martini, Gordon's gin . . . stirred, not shaken."

"With all due respect to Bond, James Bond, of course."

"Oh, absolutely. And speaking of Mr. Bond, I understand that some years ago you purchased at auction the steel-rimmed bowler hat belonging to the character Oddjob from the movie *Goldfinger*."

(The drinks are brought in and served. . . . "Thank you, Agnes.")

"Yes, that's right. Interesting that you should be aware of it. (Holding up his glass.) Cheers."

"Cheers, indeed. We make it a point to be as familiar as possible with the purchase history of our competitions' clients. Especially those clients who, how shall I put this, who exhibit rather peculiar . . . no, let's say, *unique* tastes."

"Well, to tell you the truth, Miss Worthington, my tastes are quite conservative."

"Really? (She opens up a gray, cloth-bound folder lying in front of her on the desk, and begins to read off a list of items.) Six life jackets from the *Titanic*. Al Capone's baseball bat. Hemingway's double-barreled shotgun. Gandhi's enema bag. Sylvia Plath's oven. A box of soap produced at Auschwitz. And my personal favorite, the pink, blood-stained dress last worn by the then Mrs. Jacqueline Kennedy during a brief, though memorable visit to Dallas, Texas. Now, with all due respect Mr. Franklin, this purchase history of yours would suggest that your tastes are either anything but conservative or that you subscribe to a school of conservatism with which I am unfamiliar."

"My, I am impressed. You people do your homework, don't you? And yes, I can certainly understand your, ah . . . your confusion. First of all, let me correct you on one minor point. The dress which you refer to was not last worn by the late Jacqueline Kennedy-Onassis."

"No?"

"No. In fact, it's been worn several times since Dallas, and the week after next, it's going to be worn again."

"You're joking!"

"I most certainly am *not* joking. When I said earlier that my mind was elsewhere, it was in reference to this upcoming occasion. And, it's for this occasion that, for the tidy sum of 157,750 pounds, your firm has had the good fortune to get rid of that soccer jersey."

(Speaking into the intercom: Miss Worthington says, "Agnes, another round of adult beverages, please. Make mine a double, thank you.")

"Mr. Franklin, my confusion to which you recently alluded grows in leaps and bounds. If the matter isn't of an extreme level of confidence, would you mind explaining yourself just a tad?"

"No, I don't mind explaining myself. In fact, I often find it therapeutic. The identity of my clients is highly confidential. The nature of my business, on the other hand, is what you might describe as one of those open secrets. I am fairly well known amongst a certain class of people."

"What class of people might that be, sir?"

"Well, to put it bluntly, it is that class of people who, essentially, have no class. The world, of course, is crawling with them. Fortunately for me, however, many of these people do have a great deal of money, and because they are so utterly boring and so dismally incapable of generating interesting conversation, they often rely upon their material possessions to speak for them. Your business, Miss Worthington, caters perfectly to their needs."

"I beg your pardon, Mr. Franklin, but I think we have some very interesting clients. Clients who I imagine are quite capable of generating compelling conversation."

"You *imagine*. Have you actually met any?"

"Why, yes. Yes. I'm sure that I have."

(To the intercom: "Agnes, dear, how are you coming along with those adult beverages. . . ? That's a good girl.")

"Now let me see. . . . Yes, a most distinguished looking gentleman. . . . Was it last week? No. It was . . . it was. . . . Oh, Agnes, there you are. (Miss Worthington drains half the martini in one gulp.) Ah, that's so refreshing. Very well stirred, Agnes. Very well stirred, indeed. One of your better efforts I should say. Agnes has a marvelously limber wrist, Mr. Franklin. Great for stirring. You don't knead bread do you, dear. . . ? No, of course you don't. Bread kneading builds up too much muscle mass in the wrists, which impedes the supple agility required for artful stirring. Yes, that will be all for now, dear. Do stay within voice range though, thank you so much."

"Cheers, Miss Worthington."

"Oh, absolutely. Cheers, Mr. Franklin."

"You were saying. . . ."

"Was I?"

"About one of your *interesting* clients. A most distinguished-looking gentleman that was here recently, although apparently not last week."

"Ah yes . . . yes. I believe his name was Koorstra. He was Dutch. He purchased a painting by the American Impressionist, Mary Cassett."

"A still life, no doubt."

"That's correct. A bowl of fruit. A bowl fruit resting upon a table, as I recall. Not the sort of thing that one would be likely to come across in your portfolio."

"I appreciate some of the Impressionists. Not Mary Cassett, particularly, but others. I do happen to own a couple of Francis Bacon's works."

"Somehow that hardly comes as a surprise to me, Mr. Franklin. Brilliant artist, of course, but tending towards the macabre. I wouldn't fancy waking up to the sight of one of his paintings every morning. Now please, if you will, continue telling me where your mind was straying with regard to Pele's jersey and Jacqueline Kennedy's pink dress."

"I thought you were going to tell me why this Dutch gentleman was so interesting. . . . Ah, never mind. Perhaps later. Obviously, all rich people are not boring. I just happen to have made a great deal of money catering to those who are. My particular focus is upon a subgroup of boring rich people. Namely, boring rich people who can think of nothing better to do with their time than indulging in bizarre eccentricities. The list of items that you read off earlier are all for rent. I rent them out for a considerable sum of money. The pink dress and the Pele jersey, for instance, are being leased for an evening by a wealthy couple of male homosexuals. They're hosting a masquerade frolic next month somewhere in Amsterdam. One of them is Dutch, although I seriously doubt it's the Dutchman of your acquaintance. My Dutchman would have little use for a still life painting of a bowl of fruit, regardless if it were resting upon a table or not. He and his mate are boring rich people with extraordinary sexual appetites of a most eccentric nature. In fact, if frequent-flyer mileage benefits were awarded to genitalia, these two cocksuckers would be on Mars by now."

"I shudder to think of what use some of the other items on that list . . ."

"Best not to think along those lines, Miss Worthington. I can tell that you are a young woman of delicate sensibilities."

"Al Capone's baseball bat?"

"My goodness, Miss Worthington, you *are* shuddering. Perhaps I have misjudged your sensibilities."

"Why, Mr. Franklin, what on earth could you possibly mean by that? Honestly!"

"Forgive me, Miss Worthington. I suppose a man in my line of business tends to become rather jaded after a while. Although, if you don't mind my saying, you do have quite an alluring shudder. Is it something you practice, or does it come naturally to you?"

"I'm afraid it runs in the family. Not that it's any of your business, but my mother has been known to shudder at the slightest provocation."

"I see."

"Sylvia Plath's oven? Do you lease that out often?"

"It's fairly popular."

"Suicides?"

"Two clients have used it for that purpose."

"Successfully?"

"No. Failed attempts on both occasions."

"I have no respect for people like that. It seems to me that regardless of how depressed people may be as a consequence of their miserable and incompetent lives, they should at least be able to kill themselves without mucking things up."

"Well, you're a woman of high standards, Miss Worthington. I admire that. As for the oven, it's mostly used for small, private dinner parties. I understand that it's very good for casseroles and chicken pot pies. Soufflés are another matter. One client had to pay a hefty restoration fee when her soufflé aux champignons exploded."

"What a shame. I just adore champignons. They're mushrooms, right?"

"They are in France, yes."

"Well, Mr. Franklin, I suppose we should proceed to the business at hand. I understand you'll be presenting us with a cheque drawn against an account you have with Barclay's Bank here in London."

"That's correct."

"Very well. I'll just have Agnes bring in your purchase, now. Would you care for another Scotch and soda?"

"Sure, why not?"

(To the intercom: "Agnes, dear, please bring in the Christie's cardboard box. I believe it's the one on the shelf behind your desk. And, while you're at it, two more adult beverages, if you please. Thank you so much, dear.")

"Agnes is such a peach. Marvelously attentive young girl. I'd be positively at sea without her."

"She looks familiar."

"Does she now?"

"Yes, but I can't place her. Oh well . . ."

"Interesting. You may, however, have her confused with someone else. Agnes spent her formative years attending convent schools in Switzerland. Her father was an extremely successful currency trader. Then, unfortunately, things started to go terribly wrong. His wife—Agnes' mother—drowned in a yachting accident while they were cruising the Greek islands. Shortly thereafter the father lost everything in a trading scandal and committed suicide."

"Successfully, I assume."

"Yes, but then he was part German. They're a competent race."

"Often boring, though."

"True. I think it has something to do with their language. Even on those rare occasions when they do have something interesting to say, it still sounds dreadfully tiresome."

"Unlike the French, for example."

"Exactly. A Frenchman could describe a day in the life of his pet sloth and make it sound fascinating. Anyway, poor Agnes has been orphaned and fending for herself since she was 17. She's now 24 and . . . ah, here she comes. . . . Agnes, you might as well have the honor of presenting Mr. Franklin with his purchase. That's a good girl. You can go freshen up now if you'd like, dear. We'll be wrapping up business here shortly and then I have something special for you to . . . to exercise that marvelously limber wrist of yours."

(Agnes exits with a bit of a shudder and a slight blush forming upon her cheeks.)

"Pardon me for making the observation, Miss Worthington, but the young lady seems to have a similar shudder to your own."

"Really? Well, perhaps there's something contagious about it. Ha!. Anyway, cheers, Mr. Franklin. If you'll open up the box, I trust you will find the foot . . . the soccer jersey in sparkling condition and ready for a frolic on that pitch of a different sort to which you referred earlier."

(Mr. Franklin opens the box, and stares for a moment with a bemused look on his face.)

"Well, my, my . . . what have we here?"

(He thereupon holds up a spiked, suede bra with matching panties and a leather whip.)

"Oops!"

(Miss Worthington begins to shudder uncontrollably.)

"And that, dear audience," said Genevieve, "is as far as it goes for the time being."

"Well, bravo!" said Sean. "I think I may have heard that Dutchman's confession once."

"Which Dutchman?" I asked. "Miss Worthington's client or Mr. Franklin's?"

"Mr. Franklin's Dutchman, laddie. I'm afraid that being a bore is not classified as sinful behavior by the Catholic Church."

"Perhaps some time when you're up in the pulpit sounding off, you might propose that it should be," I suggested.

"That's not a bad idea, Mac. I'll keep it in mind. Anyway, I enjoyed the sketch, Genevieve, and very well done by your most capable thespians."

"Oh, it needs a lot of work but we're going to have fun with it. Now, I don't know about the rest of you, but this ol' one-legged madam is past her bedtime. Mac, it's been a hell of an evening. I wish you many happy birthdays to come, but I hope you'll consider this one to have been memorable."

"Absolutely, Genevieve. Many thanks . . . many thanks to all of you."

Genevieve then presented me with one of her Lalique brandy snifters as a birthday present, and as I rose to say good-night, Sean christened the crystal vessel with a generous dose of Jameson for my voyage home.

"Take the matchstick with you," he said. "Use it to light up that other Cohiba I gave you."

As I walked out of the suite, along the hallway, and down the stairs, it occurred to me that I had no idea where Genevieve, Jeanette, and James were staying. Maybe Genevieve would take up Sean's offer to spend the night with him. Maybe they all would. Like the woman said, it had been one hell of an evening. But I was glad to be alone again.

Outside on the garden terrace below the Author's Suites, I sat on a rattan sofa. There was no one around. Just me and the crickets. It had to be nearly three o'clock in the morning. A couple of ground-level lights bestowed an enchanting amber complexion to the green palms and shrubs. The misty air was fragrant with the sweetness of frangipani. Barges, dark hulks in the distance, glided gracefully in the moonlight upon the river. Little waves lapped gently against the stone embankment. Cradling crystal breasts, I sipped my Irish whiskey. Oh yeah, it had been one hell of an evening. Only thing that could have made it better would have been to have had my father with me. I must have dozed off thinking about him. . . .

―――

Next thing I knew, there was a hand on my shoulder and a concerned-looking face above me. According to a badge on the breast pocket of his uniform, that face belonged to the night manager of the hotel.

"Khun Mac," he said. "Khun Mac, are you all right?"

"Just fine, thanks," I said. "Sorry, I must have fallen asleep."

"No problem, sir. You're not staying at the hotel, are you?"

"Wish I was, but it's a bit out of my budget, if you know what I mean."

"Certainly, sir. Out of my budget, as well. One of our security guards tried to wake you earlier. When he was unable to do so, he came and got me. Terribly sorry to disturb you, but I'm afraid it's against hotel policy . . ."

"To allow drunken vagabonds to spend the night passed out on the hotel premises?" I said, sitting up with a grin on my face.

"Ha! I wouldn't put it like that, Khun Mac. It's just that . . ."

"I understand. It's quite all right. Tell me, how is it that you know my name?"

"Khun Sompong, he's a good friend of mine. When the bar closes we usually have a drink together while he's cleaning up, and he tells me about the highlights of the evening."

"You mean, assuming there were any."

"That's true, sir. It would seem, however, that last evening's highlights made up for quite a number of evenings when there were no highlights to speak of. It is my understanding that you were a witness to all of them. . . . Oh, and happy birthday to you. Sompong told me that you and your party appeared to be having a fine time."

"We had a wonderful time. And no small thanks to Sompong, himself. He was a marvelous host."

"He most certainly is. We are so pleased that you all enjoyed yourselves."

"What is your name, by the way?"

"My name is Martin."

"Interesting name for a Thai."

"My father was English, sir."

"*Was?*"

"He passed away some years ago."

"Sorry. So did mine."

"Ah."

"Well listen, Martin, you mind if I stroll around the garden here for a while before I leave?"

"Not at all, sir. Take your time. I'll arrange to have one of the hotel limousines give you a lift home when you're ready."

"Oh, I think I better take the skytrain."

"The skytrain won't be in service for another hour or so. Besides, the limousine is on us—no charge. We'd be very pleased if you'd consider it our birthday present to you."

Ah, the joy of little gracious gestures, I thought to myself. This is why the Oriental is so often considered by so many people to be the finest hotel in the world.

I strolled around the garden thinking of Conrad and Coward and Maugham . . . imagining what the place must have been like when it was simply known as a 'seafarers lodge.' Out upon the terrace along the river, I stood while the sun began to rise behind me. Then into the River of Kings I decanted what remained of my Irish whiskey.

The limo was waiting for me as I walked out the lobby doors. It was a cream-colored Mercedes sedan with the Oriental logo on its side. A smartly dressed chauffeur opened the back door and I nestled in on the leather seat.

"Sukhumvit, Soi Nana," I said.

"Yes, sir. And, Khun Mac, if you'll slide open the cabinet in front of you, you'll find a gift from Khun Sompong."

It was a bottle of Jameson.

"Mind if I smoke?" I asked.

"Not at all, sir."

I poured a bit of the whiskey into my crystal glass and lit up the Cohiba with Sean's matchstick. A tinted skylight purred open on the roof of the limo.

"Driver," I said, "how about we take the long way home."

"No hurry?"

"None whatsoever."

"Very well, sir. The long way home it will be."

What the hell—it was still my birthday in Chicago.

More Amusing Musings from McFinn . .

Ever Felt Like Cashing in Your Chips and Moving to a Tropical Island Paradise? Well, our Man McFinn Did Just That . . .

In dread of waking up one morning twenty years on, with nothing to show for himself "other than one busted marriage, two unpublished manuscripts, three career changes, a four-bedroom house, a five handicap at golf, and a six-figure income," McFinn decides to go on the bum and scratch his itch for authorship . . . quitting the job, selling the house, kissing the old lady, and kicking the dog on the way out.

And so, slipping out of the Chicago Loop, our hero—reinvented as beach-bum philosopher, humor writer, restaurateur, newspaper proprietor, and maverick-at-large—retreats to the idyllic tropical shores of Koh Samui, making his new home a rustic bungalow "*in a seaside compound for impecunious tourists, tramps, vagabonds, and the occasional fugitive....*" Most stay a few weeks, but no one stays longer than he does.

Out of the Loop chronicles McFinn's humorous adventures and misadventures as he ponders the world from his verandah, encountering assorted bums, bores, boors, and beautiful women (with varying degrees of romantic success and disaster) along the way.

"As [his] dear old grandmother used to say,
'You made your bed; you sleep in it.'
She was one tough cookie, that broad."

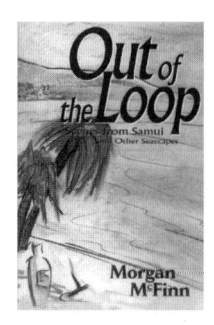

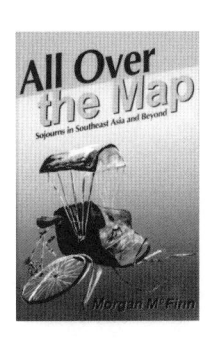

The World's Most Committed
Leisure Activist Takes to the Road . . .

A year after the publication of his paradise journal *Out of the Loop*, slacker *extraordinaire* Morgan M̊Finn finally relinquishes his hammock on the glorious shores of Koh Samui in the Gulf of Siam. In an attempt to widen his orbit of earthly experiences, M̊Finn sets off to other exotic locales around Southeast Asia and even further afield. Taking up residence in a series of charming hotels, he attempts, as usual, to make himself as comfortable as possible .

Several sojourns take our man to Phnom Penh, where he stays at the Hotel Paradise, hobnobs with members of the expat community, and undertakes a daunting philanthropic enterprise. On an island in Greece, he stays at the Hotel Rex, visits his old friend the "hermit-poet" of Patmos, and wades through the choppy waters of two holiday romances. At the Hotel Rockholm by the Arabian Sea in Southwest India, M̊Finn does his best to rekindle the pleasures of a bygone era when the British Raj were the toast of the town. And in the midst of all this, our boy even manages to inject some action and suspense into his idle and idyllic lifestyle—by planning a murder in Marrakech

"This is the ultimate beach book. Should be installed in every beach bungalow." The Nation.

"Amusing and thoughtful prose . . . on-the-nose descriptions . . . you're likely to laugh out loud as the pages fly past." Metro magazine.

available from **ASIA BOOKS**